MW00808499

EVOLVE

RELATIONSHIP DYNAMICS

The Revolution in Personal Evolution

By Steven DeSalvo

Steven DeSalvo
June 24, 2016

i

Copyright

Copyright © 2016 by Steven DeSalvo

Publisher: BECOME AN ADULT, LLC

All rights reserved. No part of this publication may be reproduced or transmitted in any form or by any means, electronic, mechanical or otherwise, including photocopying, recording, or stored on any information retrieval system now known or to be invented, without permission in writing from the publisher, except by a reviewer who wishes to quote brief passages in connection with review written for inclusion in a magazine, newspaper, or broadcast.

ISBN-13 (pbk): 978-0-9893465-8-0

ISBN-13 (ebk): 978-0-9893465-2-8

Library of Congress Control Number: 2015919058

Disclaimer: Reasonable care has been taken to ensure that the information presented in this book is accurate. However, the reader should understand that the information provided does not constitute legal, medical, psychological, spiritual or professional advice of any kind. This publication offers information of a general nature to support a path of awareness toward personal evolution. Should you choose to use any of the information in this publication, the author and the publisher assume no responsibility for your actions.

No Liability: this product is supplied "as is" and without warranties. All warranties, express or implied, are hereby disclaimed. Use of this product constitutes acceptance of the "No Liability" policy. If you do not agree with this policy, you are not permitted to use or distribute this product. BECOME AN ADULT LLC, BecomeAnAdult.com and related books and writings, its employees, associates, distributors, agents and affiliates shall not be liable for any losses or damages whatsoever (including, without limitation, consequential loss or damage) directly or indirectly arising from the use of this product.

Books may be purchased by contacting the publisher and author at:

BECOME AN ADULT, LCC
1001 Bridgeway #218
Sausalito, CA 95421
Email: info@BecomeAndult.com Phone: 415.413.7358

1. Self Help 2. Spirituality 3. New Age 4. Metaphysical

Acknowledgements

My sincerest thanks are given to Lee, Susan, Angel, Roger, Michelle, Gayle, Kimberly, Janet, and Tony for showing up with your love and support, and to Kali for providing inspiration. To my academic teachers who inspired me to be more than I ever imagined I could become: Dan Woodward, Patricia Hoover and Michael Collins.

Thank you to my team of editors for their tireless help:
Barbara R. Saunders, Shanti Einolander, J McCart, and Mary Beth Ferrari. It was through all of your efforts that these words came to life.

Thank you to all of the Adults in my life who have inspired me to write this book and keep me honest, and thank you to the people who have taught me the difficult lessons about growing up and learning to love myself. Thank you to those people who are in my life now, no longer in my life or no longer on this planet, for all of the lessons you have taught me. Please know that I am in gratitude for what I learned from each of you.

Table of Contents

Introduction

EVOLVE is a series of books about the discovery of the meaning of life and how we can thrive as responsible adults in a world of extreme change.

How do we go forward on this planet with seven billion people needing housing, work, and food to survive? How do we live in harmony with each other, with the earth, and with other plants and animals? We don't—unless we all do our part to make human evolution a conscious affair, one in which each of us takes responsibility for living together in harmony and peace.

A world of harmony and peace is possible. As humans we have the awareness to make our world a utopia, but only if we step up to the challenge and EVOLVE. Without this, humans could easily regress into complete chaos, foraging and killing whatever stands in the way for food and survival, much as starving apes might. We are teetering on the brink of our civilization's collapse, facing the possibility of a world in which survival of the fittest is all that matters. Accepting the diversity of expression of all human life—not just what is deemed acceptable to one class, race, or religion—will help us avoid this tragedy.

We like to take credit when life goes well, but when life does not go well, that's something else altogether. We often take a victim stance. We want to get up and walk away, and often we believe we are being victimized by life. But the truth is, no matter what emotions life's challenges invoke, we are personally responsible for our lives.

Who is a candidate for the EVOLVE program? Anyone who wants to follow a path to discover their fullest potential as a human being qualifies. EVOLVE is a tool anyone can use to recalibrate, reconnect, and retrain oneself to the true power of living.

This series presents the means for you to observe your own life objectively and see how your decisions relate to outcomes, your beliefs map to your behaviors, and your goals present as your successes. EVOLVE is a tool to see how taking back responsibility for your own life through increased personal awareness causes a shift, a shift so radical it could be considered a step forward in evolution of the human species.

If you are seeking to take back responsibility for living your life, responsibility that is often given away knowingly or taken unknowingly, then EVOLVE will bring back what you desire: a life experience where personal responsibility empowers you to effect positive change in your own life, in the lives of those around you, and in the world.

***

TRANSILIENCE

How many of us can honestly say we have not experienced at least one of the following:

- Uncertainty about the direction of life
- Feelings of being out of control
- Relationships do not work for reasons we do not understand
- Periods of depression, anxiety, or low self-esteem that are unexplainable
- Unfulfilled dreams or goals
- Being overly critical of yourself or others
- Feeling alone or disconnected
- Uncertainty regarding how to navigate change or loss
- Having a desire to change your self or change the world, but not knowing how to begin.

If you were to seek advice for any of the above, you would likely be prescribed pills or told you need years of therapy or psychiatric care to find answers and get your life back on track. Such treatments can be helpful, but often there are issues we can solve on our own to get to the root of the problem. If we are given the *tools* and the *information* that increase our awareness of when we struggle or what presents as obstacles to our growth and forward momentum, we can be empowered to find solutions to our problems. The impact of living a modern life leaves us little time to figure out what is working and what is not working in our lives. The result is that we end up emotionally bankrupt, trying to stay on track, but not really knowing which direction to turn, or where things went wrong, or even what is not working for us. Without the proper personal tools, experience, and guidance, we can wander through life aimlessly without direction and purpose.

EVOLVE gives you revolutionary new tools and ideas to increase awareness that will, in turn, help you take back control for your happiness.

You are offered the guidance, the means, and the experience to design your own *personal evolution* toward a life of joy and true fulfillment. EVOLVE presents a new way to engage with life by *increasing awareness* of all the facets of your life in which you can achieve personal change. Personal awareness leads to change, change based on the radical idea that you can take responsibility for your *personal evolution*. EVOLVE is not about evolution that is going to take millenniums to happen, but an evolutionary process that you as an individual can take responsibility for and be a part of now. The time has arrived for each of us to become personally responsible for our individual evolution, and collectively for the evolution of all humankind.

Our modern problems and chaos often result when we relinquish authority for our personal choices to others, allowing decisions to be made for us, decisions that are not always in our best interests. Over time we find decisions have gradually been made for us that all along we should have been making for ourselves.

EVOLVE is a new approach to living that not only serves our need to know how to navigate the various stages of our lives, but also shows us how to continually nurture ourselves and others through sustainable and regenerative living.

EVOLVE applies concepts related to permaculture—ideas such as observation, resilience and sustainability—not only to how we interact with the world around us, but also how we interact with ourselves, with each other, and within our communities to create regenerative systems capable of perpetual sustainability for generations to come. Every step taken toward implementing the concepts and processes presented in EVOLVE is not only a major step toward your own personal fulfillment, but also changes the lives of those around you, your community, and eventually the world.

The life-changing program offered by EVOLVE takes you back to the basics to restore that which belongs to you: PERSONAL RESPONSIBILITY. Through personal responsibility, you can discover a new way of living in harmony with yourself and with the world around you, bringing with it the enjoyment and vitality of life and the peace of mind to know what you desire for yourself can be balanced with the needs of others.

Note to Reader:

The books in EVOLVE are not the result of any psychological trials or years of therapeutic experience. EVOLVE is the result of years of observing myself in my relationships with others, my successes, my failures all distilled into information that is now yours to receive. EVOLVE is what I aspire to, not where I am. I am merely human like you, aspiring to live by what I have observed, learned and written here. The first book is an honest expression of my journey into the harrowing domain of relationships, and the ensuing lessons garnered along the way. I became an observer of my own life who wanted to learn from my mistakes and successes that I write about and then share them here to help you. I do not have all of the answers, but like you, I am still seeking and learning what it means to grow up and become an *Adult*.

The writing is meant to be conversational in nature and as such is not academic so as to be accessible by a broader audience that will connect with its meaning.

This book and the related writings in EVOLVE will challenge your beliefs about how you approach and live your life. It has mine. For this reason, it can be uncomfortable at times if the information goes beyond beliefs that are outside of your comfort zone. If you experience prolonged periods of depression, anxiety, or are not able to feel comfortable with the material presented here, consider seeking the assistance of a qualified professional therapist, psychologist, or psychiatrist to assist you in this journey of personal evolution.

Why EVOLVE?

Like millions of other people, you live your life in a day-to-day routine, often supporting a system that increasingly denies the unique qualities and creative abilities that define you as an individual. Our struggle to survive in current capitalist systems leaves us little time to get to know ourselves, to know others, to know our true desires, and to understand the unique qualities that each of us brings to this world. Perhaps you are longing for something different, but you're not sure how this box you find yourself in was created or, more importantly, how you get out.

You are not alone. Millions of Americans, like millions of others worldwide, are doing the same thing: living and working in systems that sustain corporations and world powers, all the while removing the freedom and autonomy of the individual. They, like you, are asking more important questions about life and living.

"Activities" are what seem to define happiness for most people today. We think we are happy when we are engaged in activities. Happiness, however, is beyond the activities and work we perform, much deeper, and even when we feel we are happy, we may also feel something is missing or not quite right. These states of "not knowing" are times when we can get the answers we need from EVOLVE by discovering where we are blocked, where we are stuck, or where we need help moving in a new direction.

You may have reached an age or stage in your life that many consider the stage of being "adult" or "adulthood," but there is still a part of you seeking something more. Is there something more that will take you from being a supposed "adult" to becoming an actual *Adult*?

Yes, there is!

First, however, you may need help in figuring out how you got where you are. This book offers not only insights into the life you have created for yourself, but also how you can begin to contribute to a new world in which we are all valued and share in the abundance this planet offers. You want not only to survive, but also to thrive in this new world and to understand how your relationships can work beyond the chaos of complications, drama, and dysfunction.

You may want to feel more of a spiritual connection within yourself but have yet to find a religion or practice that suits your needs. Perhaps you want to discover a pace for living, one that provides time to know your true desires, or maybe you need help in discovering how money works and why it is needed. In the process, however, you may discover that what money cannot buy is exactly what you seek above all else.

EVOLVE is a system of writings and tools comprising all of the facets of your life and the discovery of how they work together. Three concepts define EVOLVE:

1. No one gave us a manual for how to become an *Adult*.
2. By learning the behaviors that define how we move from an "adult" to an "*Adult*" we can live more fulfilling lives.
3. Our evolution depends on our ability to figure out how we can thrive as individuals and envision a new world where everyone is free.

Any step taken through EVOLVE toward personal responsibility will have positive results on you and those around you. Over the long term of working with these writings and tools they have the cumulative effect of increasing your awareness, and awareness is the key to evolve! The tools offered in EVOLVE bring awareness to all areas of life that require your care and attention, and then provide the means to get you further in your journey toward happiness, health, and joy. In effect, you are being given the tools for taking personal responsibility for your *personal evolution*, and through this process you affect the evolution of human consciousness.

***

Books on self-help and spirituality are found everywhere as more and more people are seeking deeper meaning in their lives. EVOLVE takes you right to the heart of figuring out what is needed, and then gives you the tools to get you there. No one can do the work for you, but you need the tools found here to give you awareness of the work required.

It all begins with an understanding of *relationship*—relationship to your self and relationship to others and the world around us. This first book in the EVOLVE series provides a comprehensive foundation for building awareness of every aspect of relationship, including the discovery of the ten elements of healthy relationships, how we develop intimacy, the expression of our sexuality, and how to care for and maintain sustainable relationships. Also included are how to create healthy boundaries in relationships, how to recognize and manage drama, the development of conflict resolution skills, and how we decide the best possible outcomes for relationships that no longer serve us.

***

CHAPTER ONE

Reclaiming Personal Responsibility

The natural order of the universe may be one of chaos, but humans have worked throughout history to bring order to the chaos so living might make some sense to us. Many of our attempts are aimed at making us feel we are more in control of our lives. Disorder and dysfunction arise when we do not have control or things do not go the way we planned, but this is all just the natural tendency of the ego to project expectations onto life, rather than the natural humility to live in harmony with life. Until we shift our awareness away from the ego, it will continually control us and, ultimately, destroy us.

There is a trend today to subjugate people through information that fails to inform with true knowledge or to teach us what we need to know. In essence, we are lulled into deep sleep and then work tirelessly to support the systems that have put us in that sleep state. Our goal is to awaken to truth and to our authentic selves by increasing our awareness that a life thus lived is possible. A *shift* in awareness is needed so each of us begins to take personal responsibility for our awakened consciousness.

One way to shift our focus away from ego-centered living is through *self-observation*. Self-observation is the process of observing our thoughts and emotions, and then observing any actions or behaviors resulting from those thoughts or emotions. The process of self-observation is what allows us to move to a new state of awareness and to make lasting changes in our behaviors and how we live.

Before we get to any new state of awareness, we first have to take the necessary steps to set the stage for something new to occur. The magic happens when we open ourselves to new possibilities. What's interesting about the stage we are setting here is we observe the drama gradually unfold, fold back on itself, and completely disappear.

***

Self-observation begins now as you read the following scenario:

You are invited to a play, but what the play is about is not disclosed to you in the invitation. Your ticket is provided and only one request is made: you must watch this play from beginning to end without leaving. You agree to these conditions.

Now, imagine yourself walking into the theater. At first, the stage is dark, and then the curtains come up gradually, revealing a stage set ready for a scene played by actors who are now assuming their places and roles. As the curtains open and the story unfolds, the play is a series of scenes that each show a current point in time as an adult, and then a flashback to the point in time as a child or young adult who gave shape to what is being portrayed. As the play begins to unfold, it all starts to feel very familiar. At a certain point you realize this story includes all of the significant events in your own life— the painful events as well as the joyful ones. The complex cast of characters enacts all aspects of yourself: the hurts, the pains, the happiness, and the sadness. You observe how all your significant relationships came in and out of your life, as well as your repetitive patterns in relationships, both healthy and destructive. The flashbacks portray exactly where the seeds of all your beliefs and behaviors originated and took form, but to see it all presented objectively on this stage with you as the observer gives you more insight, insight into yourself and into your beliefs.

At first it feels strange, but these feelings grow to include confusion and shock as you watch your life being played out right in front of you with everyone in the theater watching.

It all feels so uncomfortable that at several points you almost decide to break your agreement to watch it and are tempted to leave. But as you continue to watch, you see yourself start to shift from reacting to what is being presented to watching it more intensely with detachment and curiosity. You

2

see yourself objectively with *Detached Perspective* as you watch all the characters from a distance play out your life, and you start to see how all your hopes, fears, and desires became your goals, successes, and failures.

As you continue to watch the story unfold with more objectivity and detachment, you start to become more engaged with the story, *your* story. As the story progresses, you can see how all of your choices and decisions, both bad and good, have led up to this point right now and have formed the you who walked into this theater. You see that it was all perfect, neither bad nor good.

Now you can see the motivations behind your actions, how they led you down certain paths, and even how you avoided responsibility for what was happening in your life. All along, all the lessons you needed to learn were presenting themselves, and for whatever reason at the time of presentation it had not been clear that a gift was being given. The only thing missing during the pivotal moments in your life was the ability to consciously and objectively observe what was really happening and how it might affect you and others. If you had had the awareness to make better decisions, then you would have made different decisions—and better choices.

You come to the current point in time of observing your life on stage and realize the life portrayed before you has arrived at the exact point where you walked into the theater. The play ends on stage, but your life will be different when you leave. In fact, it feels in some sense that your life is just beginning. You've seen your life up to this point portrayed on that stage, and now you want to actively engage in changing your life going forward.

How do you make this lifetime the best performance you can? This is the question now living in you.

***

EVOLVE is about setting the stage for you to participate in the grandest theater production ever imagined: the theater of your life. And now you are conscious that you are the director of the play. In this new life, you know where the boundaries of the stage lie, how to set the stage with the scenes that support you, and which characters play key roles with you on that stage.

With more awareness of how you got to now, from this point you can see how to take full responsibility for how your life unfolds going forward. Personal responsibility is about making the effort to increase your awareness now so you can make better-informed decisions for living your life as you move forward. Now, you can take responsibility to write the script of your life: the central themes you want to play out; how the participants enter and exit; how the mood is set in each scene; and even how you choose to end this story of your life. EVOLVE will take you to the goal of personal responsibility and awareness.

The EVOLVE Audit

Answer the questions on this list, and make a note of your "yes" answers.

- Have you ever wanted to say "Grow Up" to other adults?
- Does something seem off in your life?
- Do you experience periods of depression or sadness without understanding the cause?
- Do you ever find yourself feeling alone or lonely?
- Do you believe other people have it better than you?
- Do you get pulled into other people's drama?
- Do you wish for a better life for yourself?
- Do your personal relationships enrich your life experience?
- Is there drama or dysfunction in your relationships?
- Do people respect your boundaries?
- Do you have a hard time respecting the boundaries of others?
- Do you desire to be a parent or want to be a better parent?
- Do you have difficult relationships with your family?
- Do other people not meet your expectations?
- Are you single and would like to initiate a romantic relationship, but feel you don't know how?
- Do you find you are not able to sustain healthy relationships with others?
- Do you give too much to others and often find yourself depleted?
- Do you fail to keep your commitments to others?
- Do others fail to keep their commitments to you?
- Does the world feel overwhelming or chaotic?
- Do you have difficulty making decisions?
- Do you feel helpless or powerless to solve the problems of the world?
- Do you feel helpless or powerless to solve your own problems?
- Have you or someone you cared about experienced a life-threatening illness?
- Are you living paycheck to paycheck and don't see a way to financial freedom?
- Do you want to be more spiritual, but you are not sure how to make that connection?

- Are you willing to raise your consciousness if it resulted in an evolution of human consciousness?

Many of the items on this list are symptoms of personal issues that manifest outwardly as unrest and discontent. It's hard to find anyone who doesn't answer "yes" to at least one or two of these questions. Some people find they have many more "yes" answers than not. Whatever your response, affirmative answers to more than one of these questions indicates you would benefit highly from EVOLVE, which has been proven to improve and help solve these issues and many others.

EVOLVE is not a magic bullet. It is not designed to address every life circumstance you encounter. It is designed as a jump-start that gets your life back on track through the writings here and through self-observation, helping you to engage with life in more healthy ways. More importantly, it gives you the knowledge and awareness in certain areas of your life needing your attention to get them back on track to health and happiness. Once you have completed any book in EVOLVE, you will discover changes in your life that positively affect you and eventually those around you. EVOLVE can then be used to create an ongoing plan of well-being that can lead you to true happiness and peace. All it takes is a willingness to read these pages and an openness to new ideas that result in change: changes that improve your life.

Becoming a *Real Adult*

There are five ways we interact with life: through our senses, through our thoughts, through our actions and behaviors, through our relationship with ourselves, and through our relationships with others. How we choose to engage with life in each of these five areas determines our peace and happiness. Our peace and happiness are determined by the level of awareness we achieve in each of these five interactions with life.

We come into this lifetime with trauma from our births, or through our life experiences we become injured and find we may need healing at the emotional level, the psychological level, or the physical level. My own quest for healing at the emotional, spiritual and physical levels led me to discover what it meant to be a happy, healthy, and thriving *Adult*.

Reaching the *age* of adulthood as an adult is different from reaching the stage of maturity I term *Adult* with a capital "A." Reaching the *age* of adulthood is not necessarily reaching the full awareness and maturity of true *Adulthood*. This distinction is used throughout the book to delineate between the two.

Most people perceive becoming an *Adult* as some kind of burden that is not fun, that removes our playfulness or spontaneity. The definition I am proposing of *Adult*hood is a person who has figured out how to engage with and navigate the major areas of life in healthy constructive ways, thus achieving freedom from the dysfunction of life. Along the way such an individual finds that happiness and spontaneity are actually always present and available. One does not exist just *living,* but actively engages in life *thriving*.

Becoming an *Adult* is not an artificial standard of superiority to which we adhere that means we do not have fun or we do not enjoy life. Contrary to this, becoming an *Adult* is about removing the behaviors and beliefs we learned from family and social contexts, which we find are actually now in the way of living purposeful and fulfilling lives. When we approach life as an authentic *Adult*, we step out of the *drama* and *dysfunction* that cause suffering for us and for others. We free up energy that was spent living life having to struggle and instead find new paradigms of living to becoming peaceful and harmonious. This newfound energy can then be applied to other forms of creativity and doing what we love.

Life becomes fun and joyful again when we are not weighed down by drama, dysfunction, and difficulties of life as an adult, and when these do come up, we have the tools to work through them…as an *Adult*!

EVOLVE is about going a stage further from what we previously considered adult and stepping into a new paradigm that represents a shift in

7

ur thinking and being to become all we were destined to be as *Adults*. When we become *Adults*, we are prepared for all the changes that occur in our lives, and there are going to be many.

With EVOLVE we learn how to live in these turbulent times within a toxic world. But more importantly, EVOLVE supplies the tools to reactivate life to its fullest potential in the face of change and uncertainty, giving us deeper meaning, greater purpose, and renewed confidence restoring our lives to peaceful, happy, and purposeful existence.

While change is inevitable, when we take back responsibility for key areas of our lives, we gain the confidence to deal with the changes that are continually occurring to us and around us. When we hold on too tightly to what we think we know or what we expect, we stifle our ability to grow, change, and ultimately to EVOLVE.

When we step into our full potential for the first time in our lives and experience what it truly means to live life fully, we can begin to take full responsibility, individually and collectively, for our conscious evolution. Gautama Buddha's words were interpreted to say "No one saves us but ourselves. No one can and no one may. We ourselves must walk the path."[1]

Within each of us is a treasure of gifts we offer the world. Discovering that treasure is about digging deeper into one's self and uncovering what "is," which is already and always there. These skills aren't magic, but neither are they obvious, or we wouldn't see the chaos and separation that exists in the world today.

When we do not realize our full potential, it is as if we are under water without any way to resurface and see the light of day. This manifests as having no clear direction, feeling our lives are meaningless, and feeling disconnected from our selves or others. For some, the water is deeper and murkier. For others, there may be occasional glimpses of that light we are trying to reach; however, once we begin to realize our potential and get more

---

[1] Dr. Paul Carus. "Karma, A Story of Buddhist Ethics." 1894

clarity, we can fully place ourselves on a path that enables us to navigate our lives differently.

Evolutionary Transfiguration

Self-help books and modern spirituality have tried to bring us to the peace and happiness we seek. Yet we still find ourselves blind to how we apply an actual value system that works for everyday living in this modern world. With EVOLVE we learn new skills and techniques that can be incorporated into daily life and that serve us now and in the future. We look at specific behaviors while increasing our awareness of interactions with others and the surrounding world. The shift in perspective we experience is revolutionary in its ability to transform us into *Adults* who not only exist but also live in self-fulfillment. Without learning these tools, we continue to wonder why our lives feel out of sorts, disharmonious, or unhappy. With these tools, an *Evolutionary Transfiguration* is possible that truly helps us to evolve to higher levels of awareness and *being*. Only through the mechanisms of increased awareness and commitment to personal change can a higher level of self-responsibility emerge that collectively will change the world.

Transfiguration is the state we seek and the state we are capable of achieving. Our transfiguration is met when we fully engage in the process of utilizing the tools of EVOLVE to evaluate, self-reflect, realign, and execute. Information, work, addictive behaviors, and substance abuse have lulled us into a dream state in which we do not even recognize how unhappy we are . . . until we start to awaken to what living can become when we are truly alive and aware.

The word "transfiguration" is from the Latin *transfigurationem* (nominative *transfiguration*) and means "a change of form," in this case from one type of human being to another type of human being. The change from an adult to an *Adult* is that extreme, that distinct.

Throughout the series we see this as a shift from yourself to *yourSelf*. This transformation from merely knowing ourselves as a body, a personality, and a mind to experiencing the truth of ourselves as a vessel of vast, eternal love with infinite potential is what we seek, no matter what age we may choose to seek it or even if we're not consciously aware that we are seeking it.

At the heart of this transformation is our capacity for intimacy and our ability to show up in our relationships with transparency and undefended love. In today's complex world we have become to some degree disenfranchised from ourselves and from each other, and therefore the need for intimate relationships has never been greater in the evolution of humankind. We are at a critical point in time during which we must evolve as a human species so we can live together in harmony with ourselves and with the planet. Without this evolution, we face possible extinction of the human species, or at a minimum extreme changes in the way we live going forward.

CHAPTER TWO

Healthy Relationships

The first book of the EVOLVE series, *Relationship Dynamics,* shows us how we can re-establish the direct connections we seek with the people and the world around us to bring us back into balance with the most important aspect of living: our relationships.

When we stop and ask ourselves why we feel empty or what is missing from our lives, we realize our immediate *connection* to the world around us has been removed. Instead, we are connected through devices that tell us how to experience the world around us, or newsfeeds that tell us what we are to believe or how we are to engage. We have also accepted living in a society of distraction, and moving from one distraction to another has become the norm for how we believe life is to be lived.

Relationships necessitate a shared language for how we are to navigate how we engage and communicate with each other. Without a shared common language, we do not have a foundation from which we can agree on how we are to engage with each other. *Relationship Dynamics* provides the common foundation and language from which we can build lasting and resilient relationships.

Through our relationships we see the reflections of our priorities and values. We look at not only the elements of healthy relationships, but also the dysfunction preventing us from experiencing our full ability to relate in healthy ways with others. Each of us has areas of strength, and areas of weakness that require more of our attention. The areas we will look at include:

✓ Developing deeper intimacy through effective communication
✓ Assessing how we make and keep commitments to one another
✓ Realizing how drama affects our interactions
✓ Identifying and resolving conflicts

✓ Setting and respecting boundaries

✓ Managing expectations, assumptions, and projections

✓ Learning how respect and trust affect our position of influence

✓ Realizing how judgmentalism affects us and our view of others

These skills are not solely focused on relationships with others, but also include the most critical relationship of all, your relationship with yourself. It is from your relationship with yourself that all other relationships originate and evolve.

You will have many relationships throughout life, some for your entire life and some for only brief periods. Some relationships will end, some will restart and some will completely transform. Learning how you interact in your relationships to create long-term, healthy, sustainable, and fulfilling connections with others is the goal of *Relationship Dynamics*.

Outside of the relationship with your self, at least two people are needed to begin and sustain a relationship. Your relationships are many and varied, and if you accept each as different and bringing different aspects to your life, you enjoy each unique relationship you encounter and what it brings during your lifetime.

Friends, family, and community may meet all of a person's individual needs for connection with others. Through our shared interactions and life experiences, we learn our common areas of compatibility. The areas of compatibility discovered in any relationship are the levels of shared intimacy, shared interests, shared relationships, and shared goals. Money, status and position alone do not form a basis for sustainable relationships.

There are three entities in any relationship: you, the person you are involved with, and the relationship between the two. All three entities must be cared for and nurtured at all times, or the relationship fails.

We are all continually changing, and our relationships also change over time. As we each individually change, our relationships also change, and all parties must be aware of allowing these changes to occur, while continually revisiting areas that are unhealthy or fail to serve the needs of both people and the entity of the relationship itself. The most loving thing you can do for another is to allow the space for them to evolve to whoever they are intended to be, even if this means they evolve in ways that cause the relationship to end. A relationship's value can only be measured based on the level of honesty, trust, and intimacy shared within the relationship. A given relationship does not need comparison to any other relationship to consider its value, as each brings unique and distinct gifts. While all relationships may not have the same value, everyone deserves basic decency and respect.

The best relationships occur when we feel completely free and comfortable to be ourselves, and we set others free to be themselves. The pretense of being anything other than yourself always takes more energy. Showing up as your authentic self allows a direct relationship to form. Similarly, limiting expectations of others, which in turn lessens or removes their ability to *be* or *express* themselves freely, does not serve their best interests or your relationship to them. Either pretense or expectations that limit another lead inevitably to problems both for you and for the relationship.

Rather than relating to one another as fellow human beings with reasonable expectations of living in harmony, we live in a world that encourages doing as little as possible for others rather than doing what is right and fair. Learning to have healthy and equitable expectations of one another is key to healthy relationships. When relationships become unhealthy, there is usually some associated failed expectation or an expectation that has failed repeatedly. You can only begin the process of moving your relationships to a healthier place if the people you're in relationship with are willing to make this movement with you. With this shared willingness the movement toward healthier relationships is possible.

***

13

Why Do We Seek Relationships?

Humans seek out the company of other humans for connection. Through our connections we feel validated, and our humanity expresses itself. The sense of connection we desire is the fabric of life existing within and between all living beings. Connection is our natural state of being. We are tribal by nature and created to handle life's challenges with others, rather than struggling alone. Feeling separate from our true self and from others goes against our natural state of being. Since we are in the deepest sense connected as one *Being*, we continually seek to actualize this connection with one another and with all of life to renew and restore our alignment to the fabric of life.

Through our desire for connection, we also desire to belong, to be accepted, to be liked, and to be loved. The human condition seeks relationships, some for the company of other humans with similar interests and common goals, and some simply for the pleasure of companionship. Each connection may perform multiple functions or fulfill multiple needs including emotional, intellectual, physical, social, or economic.

There are the relationships we choose, and there are the relationships chosen for us, such as our family of origin. Our family relationships are the first social structures that begin to define how we interact in relationships throughout life. No matter how good or bad life with our family of origin may have been, and whether those family members remain present in our lives or are absent, our family of origin shapes our lives and our approach to other relationships.

For some, a focus on family and a few friends may be all of the relationships needed to feel connection and intimacy with others. Others may find themselves open to many possible connections and choose to experience a multitude of relationships throughout their lifetimes.

Relationships succeed when we invest our care, our time, and our energy into them. Balancing one's needs with the needs of the other person may be an obvious requirement, but the fact that the relationship itself has needs is often overlooked. The needs of the relationship include regular communication and showing up through caring, giving support, resolving conflicts, keeping commitments, negotiating needs, and listening. When a relationship fails, you lose not only the other person involved, but also the corresponding connection of support, care, and other gifts you received from the relationship itself.

Introductions and First Impressions

If you are observant, your initial encounter with a person tells you everything you need to know about how a relationship will unfold. You only get one chance to make a first impression, so let it count and lead with your best impression. The words you choose to say in that moment and how you acknowledge and welcome another into your life create the potential for a romantic relationship or a lifetime friendship. Introductions are a time to observe a person to see how open they are to receiving you. Is there a willingness to listen? Do you find you want to hear what the person is saying? Is there a desire to engage? You can also observe openness through body language and the feelings you receive. These first interactions have an emotional quality that either draws us closer together or moves us apart. Being attuned to the emotional dynamics in introductions allows us to intuit where our next friendship or romantic relationship may begin.

We often meet people through introductions from other people, so what is the role of the person who introduces you to a new relationship? The person who introduces you is not responsible for your new relationship and how it unfolds from the point of introduction forward. Similarly, after the introduction is made, there is no further obligation by you to the person who made the introduction. The only obligation we have to others who introduce us to new relationships is to say "thank you." In business, there may be reciprocal agreements to share contacts and obligations to make introductions. While this works in business relationships, it does not apply to personal relationships and can lead to tampering into the relationships of others.

Handling introductions with care, respect, and openness brings forth the full potential from which a relationship can begin. We cannot be friends with everyone, and no one has the time to engage with everyone they meet. Knowing with whom you want to engage is about you getting clear on what is most important to you in relationships, and then having the willingness to be vulnerable and put yourself out there with compelling introductions and first impressions that reveal who you are as a person and what you bring to a potential relationship.

Your Relationship with You

The most important relationship you have in this lifetime is the relationship with yourself. You might make the argument that the only true relationship you ever have in this life is the relationship with yourself, for it is from this relationship that all other relationships originate and evolve. Your relationship with yourself is the longest lasting relationship you will have, and the only relationship over which you have any control regarding how it unfolds.

Your relationship with yourself is the rich canvas upon which you create the being you were created to be. Socrates stated this eloquently when he said, "Know thyself.[2]" He was not talking about knowing what your neighbor thinks, thinks of you, or knowing what the media is saying. Knowing thyself

---

[2] Eliza Gregory Wilkins, *"Know Thyself" In Greek And Latin Literature*. New York: Garland Pub., 1979, 286.

teaches you everything you need to know about other people and the world around you. Knowing your self is also the precursor to loving your self.

The fast pace of our lives today leaves little time to reflect on our thoughts, our words, and our actions. We can live in a state of reactivity to the demands of day-to-day life, without taking time to know oneself in the process. Engaging in relationship with yourself occurs primarily from the internal dialogue you have with yourself and its resultant behaviors. Your relationship with your own being can be anything from healthy and supportive to destructive and limiting. At some point it is important to stop and invest time in your relationship with yourself and become mindful of what you are thinking and feeling in any given moment and to observe the motivations behind your behaviors.

Do you take time to observe what you think and feel? Do you believe everything you think or feel, especially when those thoughts and feelings are based in fear, uncertainty, or doubt? How about anger, jealousy, or judgment toward others? Do your thoughts have any elements of self-degradation or harshness toward yourself? Do you judge or criticize yourself or others? Do you believe the media's or others' views about who you are more than you believe yourself? This last question and your answer are particularly important, because if you believe and trust in yourself, then you develop confidence to express what you think and feel without deferring externally to others for validation. Other people's positions and opinions matter, but no more, or less, than your own.

Learning self-observation is key to gaining a clearer understanding of who we are. Most of our waking moments are spent focusing outward on the world around us or pondering what our next move will be in the world. However, through self-observation you can turn your attention inward and inquire, "What am I thinking about right now?" "What am I feeling?" "What do I truly desire for myself?" Do your words and behaviors align with your values and beliefs? Self-observation begins the process of learning to assume personal responsibility for who we are and who we become, by stepping into full awareness of our thoughts, our choices, and our subsequent actions or behaviors.

Most people are able to observe their thoughts fairly adeptly, but fewer people are able to observe their feelings and clearly articulate them. Both are required for you to know yourself and develop a relationship with yourself. As you begin to understand your thoughts, feelings, and behaviors, you can then start to observe yourself in different interactions: "Why did I respond that way?" or "Why do I behave this way each time I feel or think this?"

You may at any time question the motives, values, or beliefs driving your behavior in any interaction. Only through this kind of observation can you decide which motives, values, and beliefs truly serve the highest good for yourself and others, and then align your behavior accordingly. Cultivating a relationship with yourself develops from deepening personal integrity, self-respect, understanding personal desires, setting achievable goals, and finding comfort with yourself and how you express yourself, either in the presence of others or alone.

All of your relationships with other people take shape and unfold from this foundational relationship of how you treat yourself. Learning to love yourself communicates to the world that you are loveable and capable of loving others. Accepting yourself without judgment allows you to be non-judgmental of others. Keeping commitments to yourself is critical to fulfilling commitments with others. Fair and reasonable expectations of yourself will cultivate your fair and reasonable expectations of others. Understanding personal boundaries allows you to honor the boundaries of others. Self-observation of our thoughts and feelings and their resultant behaviors creates a foundation of self-value and self-respect we can draw upon to navigate our lives confidently in relationship with others. Your relationship with you is the most fulfilling relationship you have if you take the time to observe it, nurture it, learn from it, and allow it to unfold as all it was meant to be.

***

Self-Value and Self-Respect

We have intrinsic value simply because we are born into human form, and this same value is granted to any life on this planet. Rather than searching for our value outside ourselves, we realize our value is divinely given and always here. Seeking external validations of ourselves through other people, through our jobs or in the world around us, clouds our ability to find the peace of knowing our true self-value. Developing self-love, self-trust, and self-respect allows us to build a personal image of self-worth. This self-worth cannot be disrupted by others or by the adversities life presents us.

The foundation for self-respect develops through responsible behavior toward self and others. First, your thoughts, words, and actions must come into alignment with your intent, and then your behaviors begin to reflect that intent. Getting to know yourself through this alignment by integrating those behaviors that serve to support and nurture your personal well-being, while discarding those behaviors that no longer serve you, is another milestone toward becoming an *Adult*. This support includes loving yourself when you succeed and being even more compassionate and loving to yourself when you fail. If you beat yourself up and hang on to your past mistakes, you do nothing but take energy away from living the fulfilling life you were meant to live. This doesn't mean you don't take responsibility for personal mistakes or mistakes involving others. Becoming a responsible *Adult* means you are responsible for the choices you make, and you are able to mindfully observe the corresponding results of those choices and make amends when needed. This observation requires you to stop, look at perceived mistakes, take corrective actions, and commit to avoid repeating the same mistake while letting go of harboring any feelings which limit your potential. Our ability to engage in self-reflection in this manner is one of the human capacities separating us from other sentient life forms. Self-observation is one of our greatest tools for personal evolution.

We also know ourselves by observing the commitments we keep to ourselves and to others. Keeping commitments enhances development of personal integrity and self-respect. Our tendency is to overemphasize the importance of commitments to others, often at the expense of keeping commitments to ourselves and achievement of our personal goals. The benefits of keeping these personal commitments are great, and similarly our failure to do so causes our greatest loss of momentum and opportunity in life. Learning to achieve our goals and desires with consideration for all of the aspects of our lives becomes an ever present process of making decisions from moment to moment that bring us into balance with ourselves and with others. Setting and achieving personal goals and commitments become the energetic essence of our lives in motion.

Personal Balance

Remaining balanced in all aspects of life is key to finding peace and happiness. Through self-observation of your emotional needs and physical needs, you learn when you are out of balance in your relationship to yourself and to others, and when you need time to refill or recharge yourself. We need to recharge and rebalance often throughout daily life and benefit from brief as well as longer periods of relaxation at regular intervals. This can be done by taking a personal retreat or just spending quiet time each day to reflect on how you interacted with yourself, with life, and with other people. Each of us requires balancing our personal time with time spent in interactions with others. Learning to become comfortable in being alone with yourself can help you know yourself better and provide meaningful insight into you and the world around you.

Keeping your life simple and uncomplicated can be one of the greatest gifts you can give yourself. We become out of balance when our time is overly complicated, over committed, or we try to accomplish too much. The opposite of balance is addiction and becoming out of balance often results

20

from an addiction in some form. Addictions don't only occur with the overuse of drugs or alcohol, but also in any aspect of life that takes too much time or emphasis such as work, materialism, or food. Anything in which we overindulge, overuse, or become overly attached can take us out of balance.

Accomplishing balance in our relationships begins by reducing the emotional noise by staying out of drama with others or by minimizing your time spent in dysfunctional or harmful relationships. Dysfunction occurs in relationships when thoughts, words, or actions cause suffering. The most direct removal from drama and dysfunction is to disengage, but when this is not possible clear boundaries can help to navigate these difficult relationships. The amount of peace experienced in navigating your life and relationships determines your happiness. From peace, happiness can arise. Many will seek happiness, but peace is the true state they seek through balancing all aspects of life. Life really is simple, balanced, and uncomplicated when we get out of the way and consciously and lovingly let it be.

Your Interrelationships

Interrelationships define how we interact and relate to other people in the world around us. The types of interrelationships we experience include casual acquaintances, friendships, family relationships, and romantic relationships. All of these might be considered personal relationships, or those relationships existing outside of the driving forces of money or power often associated with business relationships. Our personal relationships must be based on relationship dynamics that mutually serve the needs of those involved rather than a capitalist approach to these relationships. You cannot discount people at the expense of materialism or money.

There is a difference between a friendship and a casual acquaintance. In friendships you can ask the direct question, "Does this person enrich my life?" If you can answer this question honestly, you can determine if an actual friendship exists and what role the person plays in your life. Beyond the value of how a person enriches your life, both parties must mutually agree there is value to their friendship. Without mutual agreement and acceptance of the relationship as a friendship, only a casual acquaintance exists. This helps us to distinguish between actual friendships that are more personal in nature and relationships that are merely casual or contextual in nature. If you ask the question and discover that an individual does not enrich your life in any way, or you engage only within a certain context, then it is probably best to remain casual acquaintances or contextual friends. Your real friends are there for you in all contexts including the good times, and more importantly, the hard times. You can never have too many casual acquaintances, but genuine friendships require mutual care and nurturing to sustain.

You can have many casual acquaintances, but for a casual acquaintance to become a friend, there is more interaction and meaning to the relationship. Without this additional meaning and interaction, the basis of the acquaintance is merely contextual, *i.e.* interaction occurs in a particular context or under certain circumstances that bring you together. Deciding which relationships bring meaning to our lives is a natural process that is ongoing, changing and forever providing opportunities for new relationships, while at others times allowing the natural removal of relationships that no longer bring meaningful connections. The connections always and forever exist, but how and if we maintain our connection may change over the course of any relationship.

Our friendships become mirrors reflecting back to us who we are, what we give and what we extend outward. Your friends say a lot about who you are and what you value. If you are miserable, then your misery will love company. If you like joy and happiness, then you will have joyful and happy friends. What we desire and value most expresses itself through our friendships, reflecting who we are and where our priorities lie. Our beliefs and values carry a vibration that resonates with some people and repels others. Sensing who resonates with your vibration allows the laws of attraction to bring those who provide the most fulfilling relationship experiences into your life.

Our family of birth often establishes how we develop skills for how we engage in our adult relationships. Rarely do we get to choose the family we are born into, but we do get to choose our relationship to them as we move into adulthood. As adults, our family of birth doesn't always make real friends, because these relationships find it difficult to shift from the parent-child dynamics or sibling dynamics to the dynamics of being in *Adult* relationship with one another. Parents or siblings feel because of the connection of blood relation, the same last name, or living under the same roof, they are in some way entitled to a relationship with us, to have special privileges, or some semblance of control over us. There is often a need to unlearn how we interacted growing up in families, and to learn new healthy patterns of behavior that serve us in *Adult* relationships.

The blood relations of family do not absolve us from behaving as responsible *Adults*. These relationships are not exempt from all of the considerations and work of maintaining healthy relationships, including

23

being kind and respectful to one another, developing trust, reciprocity, integrity, and keeping commitments, as well as all of the other elements of healthy relationships we expect in *Adult* relationships.

Some of our most meaningful work during our lifetime may be to take personal responsibility for behaviors resulting from our family of birth, and to resolve our emotional baggage created by or shared with our parents or siblings. Because of similar emotional signatures we share with our birth family, our families of birth are where our adult behavior is tested most, for they often know us best and sometimes this means they know exactly which buttons to press to trigger great pain, anger, or anxiety. Your true progress as an *Adult* can often be revealed in how you interact with your family. Our families can provide a rich environment for our most meaningful work toward advancement of interpersonal skills and adjusting our behaviors toward becoming *Adults*.

Modern families have become defined not only by our blood relation, but by any unit of people that support each other, love each other, or live together through their loving care and support. Our *chosen families* are people we choose as adults who accept us for who we are and want health and happiness for us. Our best friends often become our chosen family. Your *chosen family* can become as important as your family of birth.

Our family of birth and our extended families of choice are both needed to create a nurturing connective fabric that sustains us. Shifting perception and seeing these "families" bring us connections and make us feel we belong to the tribe as "one of us" and sustains us through our lives.

Romantic relationships bring the potential for the deepest levels of connection to another, for we connect not only emotionally and intellectually, but also add the element of sexual attraction. All of us are not destined for long-term, committed, romantic relationships, but humans tend to naturally pair off together. The growth of world populations may contribute to the diminishing need to pair off because of the increased number of interactions encountered daily which fulfill an individual's social and emotional needs.

24

Significant attainment occurs in personal evolution through individual work on ourselves, but romantic relationships can be utilized for additional personal evolution and growth when the relationship shares a commitment to develop intellectually, physically, spiritually, and emotionally to actualize as authentic *Adults*.

Doing this work together is not always easy. One of the biggest mistakes made in relationships is a belief one can change another person. Too often romantic relationships start with "I love you" and then the expectation becomes "Now change." We cannot change anyone else until they are willing to change. Every person is solely responsible for changing herself or himself. The *only* control we have in any relationship is if, how, and when we connect and how we relate to another person. When you realize you do not have total control over your life, much less the lives of others, then you stop worrying about being in control and wasting energy on what is out of your control. This brings us freedom from taking responsibility for others through a perceived control we never had.

We change with time and our relationships evolve and change over time. The hope in romantic relationships is that both people change together, but this does not always happen. Sometimes one's personal growth evolves while the other person grows in dissimilar ways or at a different pace. Most optimum is when both can grow together. The greatest expression of love in a long-term relationship may be your desire for what is best for the other and their desire for what is best for you. As individuals, our true love for one another means we allow our spouses, partners, or significant others to evolve and change. We either change with them, accepting and embracing the changes as they occur, or we revisit whether or not the relationship is meant to continue in the same form. It is possible to love a person who does not desire to change or grow if the relationship contains enough meaningful connections to sustain it. If growth and changes are too extreme, and acceptance is not possible, truly loving someone can also mean you love the person enough to let them go.

25

Dreaming together as a couple is important to help shape a future together. The dreams do not always have to come true, but they give structure and meaning to the future together. Too much focus on each other or the relationship together may lead to taking one another for granted, unreasonable expectations, or continual faultfinding. The creation and focus of both individual and mutual goals can keep a romantic relationship moving toward shared dreams that serve to create the future of the relationship.

The evolution of equal rights for men and women has brought the element of equality into our relationships. Sharing work and domestic responsibilities equally requires continual compromise, communication, and consideration. These elements can be continuously revisited so living together and solving problems together is an ongoing dynamic process in the relationship.

Committed relationships are not ownership agreements. Relationships are not contracts of subjugation. We make a *choice* to commit to another person and be in a committed romantic relationship. While you may be committed to one another, this does not mean ownership or servitude in any way, for there is no desire to remove another person's freedom. True love expands within freedom.

***

Position of Influence

A position of influence from which we interact exists within any relationship. The influence of that position is equal to the level of respect and trust you have for one another. Knowing your position of influence determines how you interact and what impact you are capable of in your relationships. A balance of influence may not always exist, but the healthiest relationships find a natural balance of mutual respect and trust over time.

The level of respect and trust between two people directly affects how each hears the other person and what they hear. A healthy position of influence does not have any ulterior motive to manipulate or use another person for one's own need, but rather is built on a balance of giving and receiving information that is helpful and supportive.

The dynamics of the position of influence may be observed between parents and children, between married partners, and between managers and workers, friends, or even in the political arena between the president and the country he serves. The greater the position of influence, and reach of that influence, increases the responsibility to make the right decisions and to choose words and actions wisely.

In a relationship, the position of influence evolves as you respect and trust what another person says to you and how they behave with you. This usually means you learn to trust others because they tell the truth when they speak and their behavior matches what they believe and say. Congruence is the alignment of our words with our behaviors. We become congruent when our behaviors match the words expressed. You gradually lose respect and trust when words spoken do not tell the truth, behavior is out of alignment with what is said, or demeaning or disparaging words against another are used to gain a position of influence.

Your position of influence works in relationships with the following dynamics. If you don't respect someone, then you probably will not trust them. If you don't trust a person, then you probably will not listen to what they have to say or care about the meaning of their words. Without trust and respect an individual's position of influence with you will be low. Similarly, if you don't speak the truth or your behavior does not match what you say or believe, then your position of influence is diminished or absent in many of your relationships.

Below is a visual representation of how your position of influence varies with the right side having more influence and the left side having less influence and how your position of influence correlates to trust and respect.

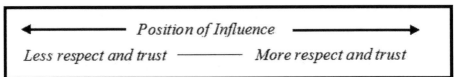

To gain a position of influence requires congruence in your values, beliefs, actions, behaviors, and words. Position of influence is not about gaining more control or power in your relationships or the world, nor about manipulating someone, but rather becoming a more authentic *Adult* who is heard and trusted in relationships. Trying to gain influence over someone through manipulation or indebtedness for money, time, or any other resource places the person in a position of servitude and fails to facilitate building a foundation of respect and trust. There are also those who may be going through difficult situations, who then use these circumstances to manipulate, gain attention, or otherwise leverage the situation to get something from you or others, thus eroding their position of influence with you. Position of influence is earned over time, not manipulated or bought.

One of the biggest obstacles to developing a position of influence may be our ego. If you or another person think you have all the answers or have it all figured out, then you are less likely to hear, respect or trust what another person has to say. Rather than assuming you have all the answers, open your self to see new answers and new possibilities.

Another obstacle to the position of influence may be the level of truth exchanged. If you are not truthful in your relationships, then there probably will not be significant trust and respect, and probably less position of influence. Personal integrity develops with others when you show up as your authentic self, not who you believe others think you should be. Through truth and behaviors that exhibit personal integrity, your position of influence naturally improves within your current relationships and continually extends to new relationships in your life. The higher the position of influence and the more people affected, the greater the responsibility for truth, decorum, and equality for all considered.

CHAPTER THREE

The Ten Elements of Healthy Relationships

We all seek to engage in healthy relationships that add value to our lives through the connection and meaning they bring. The most rewarding experience of relationship is based on the following ten elements of healthy relationships: trust, communication, honesty, reciprocity, time, compromise, shared values, shared interests, respect and support. Any of these may occur in varying degrees at any point in time during any of our relationships. Looking at each of the elements dynamically over the course of time, rather than expecting all elements to be present at any static point in time, keeps our relationships fluid and resilient. The real work of maintaining our relationships is to keep each of these areas evolving and working for everyone involved.

We look at many of these elements of healthy relationship in more depth throughout this book, but this chapter gives you an understanding of how they are connected and what they bring to relationship. Together these ten elements show us how we cherish, respect, trust, love, and take responsibility for our relationships through the associated behaviors in each of these fundamental areas.

Healthy relationships contain a high degree of transparency without the need for ulterior motives or hidden agendas. Moving deeper into any relationship is about removing barriers to understanding and knowing each other better. A healthy relationship must serve the needs of both people in the relationship, not just the needs of one. If each participant does their part by showing up in these ten areas of relationship, while avoiding unhealthy behaviors of drama, using, or manipulation, then relationships become healthy and easily maintained.

Trust

Relationships are built on trust. Trust is earned when each participant keeps and fulfills commitments, agreements and promises. Trust is also dependent upon the honesty exchanged. If truth is lacking between two people, then there is probably little trust. If truth and honesty are missing in the relationship, then trust suffers or is nonexistent. Trust is also built through intimate conversation as each person demonstrates the ability to keep personal information confidential.

Trust builds loyalty in relationships. As you become more trusting of one another, you also become more loyal. Our loyalty is usually given to those people we trust the most, and from this base of trust and loyalty, our closest and most intimate relationships evolve.

There is usually a hierarchy of loyalty throughout our relationships. At the top, many people find their spouses or significant others their most cherished and loyal relationships. Beyond this, our families and close friends receive our loyalty. Trust is another indicator for discovering your loyalty hierarchy. Getting clear on whom you value and cherish most in your life brings clear priority to those relationships most meaningful to you.

We express loyalty to another person through words, actions, and behaviors. Betrayal is the opposite of loyalty, and you can betray a person by disclosing private or confidential information, by not keeping commitments, disparaging words, gossip or by diminishing the relationship through focusing too much on others. Disloyal words or behaviors in committed or significant relationships have the added effect of diminishing the importance of the relationship to third party observers. Betrayal is damaging to a relationship if there is not clear responsibility and reparation made for any betrayal that occurs. The person or people you would call in the case of an extreme emergency may be an indication of the relationships that hold your greatest trust and loyalty.

Our healthiest relationships express a reciprocal level of trust and accompanying loyalty. Trust must be reciprocal for the relationship to maintain a healthy level. Loyalty is non-transferrable. Your focus must always be on your own personal responsibility to show up and be caring and loyal to those you care about and hope you receive their loyalty and care in return.

Consistent behavior also builds trust. When we are inconsistent or observe inconsistency in others, we become uncertain about their true intentions or how to manage our own expectations, and this uncertainty may lead to distrust. As our behavior becomes more consistent in our relationships, stability is a natural outflow. Fair and reasonable expectations add to this stability when they are delivered with consistency. When our behavior becomes inconsistent or our expectations are too great, these conditions tend to disrupt the stability of the relationship over time. It can then take time to regain trust when it has been breached or broken.

Once trust is broken, it is hard to regain. Distrust erodes a relationship and can lead to separation. Trust is regained when the commitments made are continually fulfilled so the distrust dissipates or is ultimately forgotten. Trust is continually nurtured in our relationships through fulfilling commitments we make to one another over time. We cover more on commitments in Chapter Seven.

As we continually step up, show up, and meet our commitments in our relationships, we experience the added benefits of showing our care, our love, and our respect for the other person and the sanctity of the relationship, which in turn leads to greater loyalty to one another. Trustworthy *Adults* provide their unwavering loyalty, honesty, and transparency in relationships.

Communication

Effective communication and the love and caring with which we express ourselves determine our successful navigation of relationships. The greatest human skill we can learn and master is our ability to clearly communicate and articulate our feelings, ideas, needs, and desires. The second greatest human skill that facilitates effective communication is our ability to listen and understand what we hear. Timing is important in communication because *knowing when to say something can be as important as what is actually said.* Speaking with clarity and delivering your message so that the true meaning is heard and understood by the person receiving it are difficult skills to master but worth the investment. If you do not understand something said, it is considerate to ask, "What did you mean by _____?" rather than assuming what was said, or worse yet, missing the meaning of what was said.

Our ability to communicate effectively determines the level of success we are able to achieve in all aspects of our lives, for without effective communication, we feel unheard, unrecognized, and unfulfilled. Effective communication allows understanding of our ideas, thoughts, and feelings and through this understanding we become known, heard, and fulfilled.

Communication must have a certain relevance to the present moment, without too much importance placed on the past. The best use of the past is when it serves our present moment. Communication that is based on what *has* happened, as opposed to what *is* happening, gets old over time, because it *is* old. What happens right now is fresh and relevant to both people, and the most interesting.

For effective communication to occur in relationships, it must also have the elements of responsiveness, openness, and honesty. You can be direct and honest with a person without being rude. Honest communication is clear communication with no hidden meaning. Articulating your ideas or emotions so the actual meaning of what is said is communicated is a skill which we must continuously develop, especially as we see that what is said is heard differently by each person. Any response, even if just to say "yes" or "no," shows you acknowledge the communication. No response shows a lack of respect for the relationship.

Language is ambiguous at best to express the wide gamut of human emotions. Clear communication provides clarity, removes ambiguity, and allows for a deeper connection. Say what you mean and mean what you say. Ambiguous or unclear communication creates distance and misunderstanding.

Good communication is as much about being a good listener as about clearly communicating your ideas. A good listener asks questions to clarify what is said so both people understand and hear the true meaning. By not actively listening we diminish another person's thoughts, feelings, or beliefs and make them insignificant. Everyone wants to be heard. Listening is as effective in communication as articulating ideas into words that are easily understood.

Open and honest communication deepens the bond between people and leads to lasting relationships. Withdrawing or shutting down communication by one or both people does not give the relationship the desired results for sustainability and regeneration. Both people must be allowed the respectful space to voice their feelings, thoughts, and opinions as honestly as possible. The timing with which you respond, and what is said when you do respond, show your interest and the value you place on the person and the relationship. By honoring the relationship with appropriate response time, you show not only care, but also respect for the person and that you value their time.

Taking the time to respond thoughtfully rather than simply reacting serves us better. Too often people respond quickly without thinking through the effect their response might have, especially when responding to hurtful comments or in emotionally charged conversations. A well thought out response is better than giving a response too quickly without the appropriate consideration.

The questions a person asks of us often give us more information about who they are and what they are thinking than the answers they may provide. Asking too many personal questions too early in a relationship when you meet someone is forward and invasive. A person shares more private information when trust develops in the relationship, allowing the disclosure of more personal information.

At some point in every relationship, conflicts arise. Open and honest communication is key to resolving conflicts and getting our relationships back on track. Relationships do not fail because there is too much communication, but relationships often fail without enough communication. A breakdown in communication is typically what leads to a break up in a relationship.

Communication always has a context, and understanding the context or circumstances in which something is said brings meaning of what is being communicated. You may share your views, dreams, and beliefs with each other, and even though you might not agree on all of them, you can still respect each other's viewpoint, the context or circumstances for what is said.

There are many ways for us to communicate today. Communication can be anything including eye contact, body language, text, email, phone message, phone call, or face-to-face conversation. While electronic communications with others keep us somewhat connected, no digital experience replaces the actual experience and feeling of being in another person's presence. Your undivided attention in interactions is the gift of presence with another being.

People often reveal as much meaning by what they do not say as what they do say or how they say it. In some relationships we feel connected and experience some level of communication even while completely silent with another. These are sometimes our deepest and most meaningful relationship experiences.

It is rude and inconsiderate not to respond to direct requests of communication. There are rare times when no response whatsoever is the appropriate communication. This sometimes occurs when there is a breakdown in the relationship such as during unresolved conflicts with little or no intent to work on resolution by one or both parties or an inability to do so. You can limit or stop communication when a person is being unreasonable or childish.

The most rewarding relationships we experience contain emotional intimacy, and this requires intimate communication. Through intimate communication we connect with another person at the deepest level of human experience: our feelings and emotions. Intimacy begins with effective communication, which leads to lasting relationships. Intimacy and intimate conversations are further explored in Chapter Five.

Honesty and Integrity

Healthy relationships require a high degree of honesty and integrity. Integrity is the quality of being truthful to oneself and truthful to others in our words, deeds, and actions. Our goal is to become honest with ourselves and honest with others while maintaining integrity with both.

Telling the truth is the foundation upon which lasting relationships are built. With a high degree of truth telling, agreements in relationships can be based on facts and not assumptions, partial truths, or lies. If you advocate for anything, then advocate for the truth. Truth is not an illusion. Our interpretation of truth is the illusion. Without truth, the story gets told differently, and history is rewritten to suit the needs of the storyteller. If a relationship is not built on telling the truth, then eventually when the truth does come out, it can betray the trust in the relationship. Finding out a person has lied, withheld information, manipulated, or twisted the truth can become a major setback and often a deal breaker.

Honesty and integrity are also about being forthcoming with information. Hiding or concealing information or withholding the whole truth also erodes honesty in a relationship. At a minimum, these dishonest behaviors put us on guard, and being guarded around another person takes our energy to sustain. Extreme breaches of honesty and integrity require too much guarded energy and eventually exhaust the relationship.

There are people who are not ready for the truth or do not want to hear the truth. With these people, your authenticity may be too much or unwelcome. You can only be as truthful as a relationship will allow. Honesty is not always the most pleasant thing to hear from another person, but as *Adults* we appreciate a direct and honest approach in our interactions with other people. This type of honesty with oneself and with others prevents the possibility of pain and hurt further down the road if one's true feelings are either repressed or not expressed, and the relationship unfolds based on untruths or presumption. Relationships with some level of chaos usually have a corresponding level of dishonesty occurring. Similarly, honesty and truth can clear up ambiguity in relationships and the resulting chaos. Honesty determines the basis for all of our relationships, for the level of honesty shared determines the depth of intimacy we are able to achieve with others. A conscious *Adult* is grounded in truth by using empirical proof, knowledge, or scientific data to support the truth, not hearsay or conjecture.

Reciprocity

Reciprocity is the give and take in relationships that shifts over time. Healthy relationships give and take in patterns of reciprocity that are mutually beneficial. When patterns of reciprocity are balanced, then a relationship feels vibrant and both parties feel energized and fulfilled when they come together and when they part. A relationship taking too much time, energy, or other resources away from one person or the other eventually diminishes the desire to be with one another.

Reciprocity is particularly important in the beginning of a relationship, as each person gives fairly equally of their time and resources. Asking too much of a relationship too early is a cause for concern. Reciprocity

37

continually unfolds naturally and meaningfully when both are willing participants contributing resources to the balanced reciprocity of the relationship. The ways we can give to one another are vast, but most significant contributions are communication, time given to the relationship, emotional support, and physical energy.

Generosity and kindness become unbalanced when not reciprocated in kind, and over-giving can cause as many problems as not giving enough. Finding the balance of give and take over time forms the basis of reciprocity.

In longer relationships, where the focus becomes too much about fulfilling one person's needs over the other's, the lack of reciprocity eventually fails the needs of the relationship and the needs of one or both people involved. In these relationships, patterns of reciprocity can devolve into patterns of "do-more-for-me."

Reciprocity can also be measured through the *energy* you give and receive in your interactions. Observe your energy after any interaction and ask yourself: *Have I come away with the same energy? Did I come away with more energy? Do I feel drained?* If the answer is yes to this last question over several interactions, reevaluate why you are in the relationship and what needs it actually fulfills for you or for the other person. The most rewarding relationships are those in which we come away energized by our interactions, or at the very least not drained by them. Another way to know reciprocity is through the comfort level of spending time together. In healthy relationships, you look forward to spending time together. Avoidance or dread of time together reveals the need for re-evaluation to decide if you want to continue.

There are people who make minimal investments in the relationship but expect maximum returns for their investments. They give just enough to keep you engaged, but over time you see your own investments give minimal returns. There may also be an imbalance in what is given or a feeling of obligation for what is given. Giving doesn't always have to be equal, but there is a balanced flow of giving and receiving with any resource you share, whether it is time, money, love, advice, energy, or company. We feel obliged to those people we care about, but we should not be made to feel obligated for our care.

Gratitude enhances reciprocity, so being thankful for what is given shows appreciation for the flow of reciprocity back and forth. Acknowledging receipt and expressing appreciation for one's support or gifts shows consideration and further reinforces and sustains reciprocity. When we take other's gifts for granted, the flow of reciprocity may lessen, or begin to break down. Our requests for time together in relationships must also be reciprocal. One person is not always responsible for initiating or facilitating the interactions of time together, planning interactions or invitations. We feel valued and liked through invitations, but also appreciated when our invitations are reciprocated and we are invited in return.

Give to a relationship what you would like to receive. If your needs are not met in a relationship, then ask for what you need. If needs continuously are not met, then reevaluate. Some options may include having a direct discussion about reciprocity, and potentially less interaction or suspension if the unbalance of reciprocity continues.

Giving and receiving sustain relationships. You can observe reciprocity in your own life at any moment and see what is being given to you and what you are giving. What you receive is a reflection of what you are giving.

Healthy *Adult* relationships last because those involved remain flexible and open to making the relationship work in a relaxed manner by constantly considering the changing needs of each other and the needs of the relationship. Flexibility to accept these changes and willingness to both give and receive are key elements in the success of any relationship.

Time

Time is a critical element of adult life and relationships. In youth, we tend to take time for granted and think we have all the time we need. As we reach the later stages of life, we realize how precious time is. Time spent in relationships can be the most rewarding time we experience. Rarely do people die wishing they had spent more time at work, but they often arrive at the end of their lives wishing they had spent more time with those people they love.

Relationships are developed, built, and maintained over time. How you choose to use your time together determines how your future unfolds. Look at the relationship as a whole; avoid getting caught up on one event or uncomfortable moment, but rather try to see the totality of your interactions. People often seek short term rewards in relationships ignoring the more meaningful potential of the long term gains.

Quality time spent together consists of sharing activities and intimacy or conversations mutually satisfying to all involved. As a relationship progresses, you know another person through interactions and observations of those interactions. This can certainly mean seeing the good in another person, but the "not-so-good" can be revealed as well. Is the person's intention to have an authentic *Adult* relationship, or is there another motive? Do they keep commitments to you and others? We come to know others through interactions as everyone reveals their true nature through their actions and behaviors. Given enough time people reveal themselves.

In time, you see the truth of a person's words through their actions and behaviors. When a new relationship starts, everyone is on their best behavior and putting their best foot forward. If the behavior is not the natural state of the person or who they really are, then this act of being someone else takes energy. Over time it is rare that a person can sustain the energy necessary to be someone different from whom they are. Eventually the person will revert back to their true self. It takes many interactions over time to see all of the facets of a person revealed to even begin to know them.

There is an intrinsic value to sharing time with another person, regardless of the activity or experience shared. Our time is a resource we can offer to others, as well as receive from them. In fact, time may be one of the most precious resources we have to offer, as time in this body is not long and to a large degree using our time wisely determines our happiness.

If people do not make time for you in their lives then it means one thing: other things are more important to them. This is not always personal. It can simply mean life is busy with other people or obligations, and they do not have time to devote to your relationship now. Quality time spent with others is always more important than quantity of time spent.

Our connections in relationships are continuous. Staying in touch and engaged with some degree of consistency provides the comfort of continuity that sustains healthy relationships long term. When periods of interaction become lax or too long, this often diminishes continuity. Behavior that is consistent builds trust, and eventually we become distrustful of inconsistent behavior.

Compromise

In healthy relationships, compromise is utilized to reach mutual agreements and negotiate satisfying outcomes. People give and take (compromise) in ways nurturing to both people and the relationship. A healthy relationship always has moments of disagreement, and conflict resolution reveals each person's ability to compromise for mutual solutions. People who are flexible and compromising find their relationships evolve organically and peacefully, even during times of conflict. Relationships vary in their level of congeniality from difficult to compatible, but differences can be negotiated and resolved with dignity and respect when *Adults* engage with the ability to compromise.

Compromise requires understanding you will not receive what you want all the time. Similarly, others won't receive from you what they want or desire all the time. Cultivating a reciprocal negotiation process is possible, allowing both people to express their needs and desires, and reach an agreement about what each person can actually provide for the other graciously without resentment. Sometimes your needs are met, sometimes the other's needs are met, but most often there is a mutually satisfying choice meeting the needs of both. Compromise is this reciprocal negotiation process which allows us to regenerate and sustain our relationships.

With compromise comes personal responsibility. When difficult situations or conflicts arise, each person must be willing to take responsibility for their position and compromise when possible to reestablish balance and peace in the relationship. When we can take full responsibility for all of our beliefs, actions and choices, be they good or bad, others tend to respond in kind. Rather than placing blame or judging others for mistakes made or shortcomings experienced, respect and regard are shown when each person owns responsibility for their part and willingly shows up to compromise. Taking full responsibility for all of one's actions and reactions helps a person transition to an *Adult*.

What are we compromising? Our personal time and resources are ours to give and ours to keep. The most optimum relationships are those in which there is a natural flow of reciprocity and compromise for our time and resources. If the flow of compromise becomes imbalanced, then this requires discussion and/or renegotiation to maintain the health of the relationship. A relationship cannot be on one person's terms only. Both must voice their needs, including the time spent together and personal resources shared. You meet people who are open and freely give their time and resources. You also meet self-serving people who only want to take your time, energy, and other resources with little or no return. Identifying people who know how to give, receive, and compromise serves you well in relationship to others. You become better at setting clear boundaries for the resources you have to give, allowing you to engage in healthy compromise within all of your relationships.

Shared Values

People gravitate to people who think as they do, who have similar values, beliefs, and approaches to living. Personal beliefs and values comprise our personal belief system, our foundation for living. There is a natural tendency in all of us to seek those with similar values and beliefs. While our egos form and hold our values and beliefs as true, being too rigid in our personal belief systems, or forcing these on others, causes problems and creates distance.

Values may arise from our beliefs, and beliefs may arise from what we value. Examples of major values that bring people together are integrity, honesty, respect, hard work, and kindness. For a healthy *Adult,* additional values pertaining to relationships include intimacy, transparency, truthfulness, and trust.

Beliefs are an acceptance of what we hold to be true. While beliefs may be held regardless of their verifiability or evidence to prove or disprove their truth, beliefs grounded in truth have a universal application and are more likely shared by others. Some common areas of beliefs may include a belief in God or other religious doctrines, political position, life after death, creation or evolution. We do not always have to agree on our beliefs to have healthy relationships, but our shared values in certain areas often influence the capacity for healthy relationships to evolve.

Hurtful, unloving, or unkind values or beliefs cause the greatest conflict or separation from others. Any value or belief based on love, integrity, and truth is our guide.

Values and beliefs change with time and are best evaluated on an ongoing basis. What values and beliefs are true for you at this point in time? How important is a given value or belief? Does holding too rigidly to your values or beliefs alienate or cause separation from others?

Through marketing and media, we may unconsciously value what society expects us to value, even when these values are detrimental to living a life of happiness. While we all hold that our beliefs and values are true at any given point in our lives, our values change and evolve throughout a lifetime, hopefully toward more truth and openness to new ideas. Remaining open and willing to question the truth of our beliefs and what we hold of value allows this process to unfold and further defines the values and beliefs currently most important to us.

Evaluating a particular value or belief begins by looking at all of its opposites while objectively asking to what degree each of those opposites could also be true. An example may include the judgment of a person as wrong for beliefs differing from one's own beliefs, without considering the history of how that person came to their beliefs, or how the beliefs may be true for them. One might also look at all the ways the beliefs are similar to yours, with as much emphasis given to how they are different. We can attempt to appreciate an individual's position or perspective even if we do not agree with it. The ego needs to identify with its values and beliefs, and then to believe they are irrevocably true, which causes problems to arise, creating separation rather than inclusion and understanding. Beliefs or values that are too narrow or limited, constrain or prevent a relationship from developing its full capability.

Beliefs and values can be one of the most limiting factors in relationships if they are not shared, particularly in romantic relationships. Even our choice of where we live is influenced by our desire to associate with people who have similar beliefs, values, and those people with whom we want to engage. People from different geographic regions vary in their values, their beliefs, and even their approaches to living. Finding people in a region, area, or country with similar values and beliefs to yours facilitates a life that is easier to adjust and more fulfilling to sustain.

In summary, while shared values and beliefs provide a common foundation for our relationships, how we negotiate our differences of opinions, values, and beliefs may be one of the most important skills in learning to maintain healthy and diverse relationships.

Shared Interests

Being in relationship is coming together to engage, and one of the ways we come together is by sharing experiences. Shared experiences start with shared interests, such as social activities, dining out, movies, parties, hiking, travel, raising kids, sharing mutual friends, or working together. Our shared interests provide a common ground to interact that nurtures us individually and collectively. We enjoy our shared life experiences now, and build memories that we can savor later.

People enjoy a variety of experiences, and many find pleasure in virtually anything, from the mundane to the extreme. Perhaps too often we seek sensational experiences, forgetting that each moment is filled with varied emotions, sensations, and transitions to other adventures, particularly when shared with others. We want to experience everything, from the quiet of the mind in meditation to the physical challenge of climbing the highest peaks of Mount Everest. However, for most people, a never-ending parade of adventures is not possible or even desirable. Finding a person with whom you can share life experiences that enriches the journey for each of you is most desirable. Appreciating not only each experience, but also the person with whom you share the experience brings richness to both lives. Without shared experiences, we confront the world and its wonders alone; greater pleasure and joy come from sharing our experiences with those who have similar interests.

Shared interests become the basis for many relationships. Connecting with people of similar interests brings us together with like-minded people who think and interact with the world as we do. Everything does not have to be a grand experience to be enjoyable, and sometimes the simplest experiences together are the most rewarding.

45

Some relationships seem to require a variety of experiences to keep them interesting and engaging, while others find comfort and enjoyment in the ritual of repeated activities together. The layering of shared experiences is how we come to know one another. Knowing when to keep shared experiences the same and when to seek out new experiences together is part of developing a relationship. Our shared interests provide the rich foundation from which to build a shared history of experiences together that nurtures and sustains our relationships.

Respect

Respect in relationships is a cumulative effect of many of the other elements in the relationship, including compromise, communication, honesty, reciprocity, trust, and support. The associated words, actions, and behaviors in each of these elements become the foundation upon which respect for one another is built. If these elements are not all present in healthy amounts, there is often little or no respect.

Respect can become one-sided in a relationship, but in long-term healthy relationships, the people involved have mutual respect for one another and respect for what is given and received. You respect people when you value what they say, or you value what they do, and the best form of respect exists when both are present. Respect is built on words and actions based on honesty and truth. We show respect for each other by not only what we do, but also by what we do not do.

A relationship always begins with a precedent of mutual respect, but how it proceeds from there determines how respect unfolds in the relationship. Respect in a relationship unfolds in many ways. One way to show respect is by being responsive to requests to engage, including invitations, phone conversation, emails, and texts. A response shows consideration and that you care, whether you answer yes or no, or you engage or not.

You can also show respect for another person by being fully present while *listening* and responding, and by valuing the individual's time and the time you spend together.

Another way to show respect is by respecting personal boundaries. You show a person you care for them by allowing the person to be who they are and respecting the boundaries they establish for themselves, though we may not always agree with their boundaries.

Mutual respect naturally unfolds as you learn more about another person, their values, their boundaries, their beliefs, and their integrity. Mutual respect also develops through our ability to honor and keep commitments. When people show up on time and do what they said they would do, we feel grateful, loved, and respected. Likewise when agreements or commitments are broken, we can feel betrayed, unimportant, and disrespected. Showing up for other people when you say you will is one of the best forms of respect and regard you can show to another person.

We are not entitled to a relationship with anyone because of name, past history, connection to others, or blood relationship. We earn our right to a relationship through respect and trust in each interaction in which honor unfolds. Respect is built on an established foundation of trust and honesty.

Support

Support shows caring. Through support we nurture the relationships in our lives. A level of mutual support evolves as a relationship becomes more intimate. Your family may be the first unit of support throughout your life if your relationships with family members have evolved in healthy and constructive ways. Beyond your family, developing relationships built on reciprocal support bring us the resilience we can depend upon to nurture and sustain us when needed. Support is not only about helping each other through difficult times, but also showing up to celebrate successes and good times. At some point, we all need some form of support.

Our encouragement, care, and concern for another's well-being are forms of support we can bring to others. Your reliability and dependability matter; they show your support for the people and relationships in your life that you value and cherish. The most loving and caring support we can give to another is our intentional wish for what is best for them and what will bring them happiness and joy. As fondness grows for another, you naturally have concern and care for that person's well-being. Similarly and in return, the other person feels concern and care for your well-being. This is true in every type of relationship, whether friends, family, romantic partners, or even casual acquaintances. Money is a form of support when it truly helps a person get "back on their feet" or to accomplish a goal toward independence. Without either of these or sufficient support, money may sustain them only temporarily or delay the inevitable. Money is most helpful when the decisions or circumstances leading up to any financial problems are fully understood and also addressed.

You can be willing to extend your support for others' endeavors and interests even if their interests or values aren't necessarily the same as yours. Being supportive of another person's dreams, desires, and creative ideas can be the greatest gift you can offer another and one of the greatest gifts you can receive. This type of support sets a person free to live as he or she desires, not as you desire for them. Our role is not to decide what dreams or desires are best for a person, and leaving this judgmental behavior behind allows us to support an individual in whatever way he or she chooses to live life, to achieve whatever goal or desire they decide they want for themselves. Your advice, when requested, is all you can give them, and beyond this, you set them free to choose whether they use your advice or choose a completely different path.

Supporting another does not mean telling them what to do, applying pressure for what to do, or telling another how to live their life. You are not responsible for the other's life, but rather your role is to simply support, encourage, or guide the other's choices and decisions, as long as the behaviors aren't damaging to you, to them, or to the relationship. Support does not mean you always agree with the decisions others make, but you can show your support and care, even if you disagree with their beliefs, behaviors, actions, or words.

Support is also provided when our strengths are emphasized over our weaknesses. We all have flaws and weaknesses but to overemphasize our weaknesses causes separation, not unity. We all need the care and nurturing of other humans occasionally to give us some assurance about what we are doing or where we are going. Sometimes the people who appear the strongest are the ones who get neglected when their needs arise, because they are perceived as strong enough to handle it all on their own.

Another way we can show our love and support for one another is through our consistency of assurance and reassurance. You show up in each other's lives when it matters, and you show up even when it doesn't matter, because this kind of consistency demonstrates your care, your concern, and your affection.

Our gratitude and appreciation for the gifts of support we receive is another way of showing we value the support provided. Through consistent support and gratitude you show you value the relationship and are there to provide your support in whatever way you can.

CHAPTER FOUR

What is Love?

Love is the natural state of our being, and our life's work may be to return to the pure expression of love. Love is everywhere and exists in everything, but the awareness to see it requires alignment to the love within ourselves. Once we achieve alignment, we can extend pure loving kindness outward. Love is the energy of life. We feel happy, healthy, and synchronized when united in love, and out of harmony, depressed, and uneasy when separated from love. Each moment provides the opportunity to unite or separate through the thoughts, words, and actions we choose.

Love is sacred, both in giving and receiving. You must believe true love exists before you can experience it, and until you have experienced true love, love is only an idea, a concept or an abstract feeling that is not directly experienced. True love originates from the pure heart and not from thoughts alone. True love can go unnurtured and unreciprocated which leaves it stagnant to whither and perish.

Love exists in all our relationships as the fiber connecting us. Our love is expressed in different ways depending on the length and type of the relationship. As an example, romantic love is different from the love we have for our friends or our family members, as it usually includes an expression of sexuality. Over many years, the platonic love we have for a friend may evolve to be as rewarding as any love we experience. The following words and characteristics of love described can only allude to the experience and true meaning of love:

- Love can be a mild or an intense affection for another.
- Love is free. It cannot be bought, yet the returns are infinite.
- Love persists and cannot be turned on and off at will.
- Love is boundless, endless, ageless, and timeless.
- Love is everywhere, in everyone, and in everything.

- The true nature of love is always simple and uncomplicated, not confusing, chaotic, or ambiguous.
- Acts of kindness can be expressions of love, but these alone do not define love.
- True love cannot be withheld as a punishment, nor can it be given as a reward.
- Love is always freeing, never hindering, binding, or imprisoning.
- Love is about compromise, creating solutions to problems, and finding resolution.
- Love is about coming together, not separating apart.
- Love is always patient and kind.
- Love honors truth.
- Love is expressed through equality and fairness.
- Love does not discriminate based on gender, age, race, or ethnicity.
- Love is non-judgmental.
- Love does not constrict through labels and sees beyond the labels of others.
- Love is ultimately the complete acceptance of *What Is.*

Love is not just an emotional experience in relationships; love is a verb as well as a noun, meaning it has associated actions and behaviors. The words "I love you" are lovely and easy to say, but the real meaning of these words occurs only through the actions and behaviors that are associated with the words and that complete the meaning of love. What you do and what you say continually show your love and affection for others. Saying "I love you" is meaningless without the corresponding actions and behaviors of love.

We know we love another person when we want only the best for them. We express our love by wanting happiness for them and doing what we can, when we can, to ensure their happiness. If you want to show someone your love, express it through loving words, loving actions, and loving gifts. Loving words and actions also show others how you desire to be loved. We must all learn how we want to be loved, and how others we care about want to be loved, so that love can sustain us and our relationships.

Many people love the idea of loving; they "love to be in love," but often don't take into account the true commitment loving relationships require and the ongoing commitment needed to maintain them. For this reason, love is a reciprocal process we engage in, and which we continually nurture over time. Love can move mountains when love is given at the right time and when love's full effect is received by an object of affection who is ready to receive it.

Forgiveness is another form of love that allows deeper movement into love for others and ourselves. Our forgiveness and the healing of our past hurts and transgressions allows us to trust others and to love again. Love takes bravery because in order to express love, we have to overcome our fears, vulnerabilities, and insecurities. Love flows through our being when we remove the constraints of expectation, judgment, labeling, projection, anger, and regret. When we are not able to love, we are probably stuck in some belief or state of unforgiveness of someone or something from our past. Any act of love expressed must have the genuine intent of love behind it.

Too often people want your resources or give you their resources mistaking these exchanges of needs for gifts of love. While gifts and fulfilling needs can express our love, they are only one expression of the many ways we can love. We can confuse states of being needed, indebtedness, or obligation for love, as these states engender feelings of being valued or loved. Needing someone or being needed is not true love. While we can express our love for someone when they need us, need is only one facet of loving someone and cannot be the only basis for a loving relationship.

Similarly, having expectations and fulfilling expectations can be confused for love. Having and fulfilling expectations is another expression of love, but our healthy expectations serve relationships best. Unhealthy, unfair, or unreasonable expectations require the additional burdens of constant care and attention, especially if these occur in the beginning of new relationships.

You cannot seek out love or expect another to love you, but you can love another and create the space for them to love you. Not everyone wants to receive your gifts of love and acts of kindness. Gifts of love can only be given to one who is willing to receive love. Love does not mean you are the center of someone's universe or a person's only reason for living, for true love is freeing, not binding. Developing deeper intimacy, keeping commitments, random acts of kindness, service, support, and showing up when needed are loving actions.

Love is best expressed by giving a person freedom and by not trying to change who the person is or what they choose to experience. We all want to be free to be ourselves, and to be who we truly are can be the most loving gift we can offer and receive. A gauge of the amount you are loved in any relationship is the amount of freedom and support you feel to be your authentic self rather than who someone expects you to be. Loving someone means you completely set them free and they set you free. The greatest love may be to find relationships that fulfill us with their freedom, and letting go of unloving relationships that no longer serve our freedom to evolve. We only have time and energy to live this one life, and taking personal responsibility for our life expression will be enough.

Love and commitment blind to the truth of hurtful words, actions, or behaviors is not true love and commitment. You cannot profess to love someone and then treat them in contradictory and unloving ways. People may pledge unwanted help, unsolicited opinions, or become invasive or insensitive to boundaries under the guise of love, but these behaviors are not expressions of love.

Also, love cannot make us blind to words, actions, or behaviors that are illegal or harmful to others or to ourselves. This type of blindness occurs when we love so deeply we are willing to overlook, accept, or participate in destructive behaviors. Love is always kind, but it can seem harsh when its intention is to help another through "tough love." Tough love is needed when the only way we can show a person we love them is by *not* enabling their hurtful or destructive behaviors. Love becomes unconstructive when we enable another's person's addictions or destructive behaviors with either our assistance or our apathy. Love moves forward toward wholeness. The opposite of love is apathy. Becoming a responsible *Adult* brings the awareness to discern when acts of loving kindness are needed or when tough love is needed to serve the higher good of all involved.

Most if not all our relationships experience conditional love to some degree. Having conditions on what we are willing to give in order to receive love is normal. A desire to have our needs met and fulfilled through relationships is one more facet of the human experience. While most relationships are conditional in nature, the purest love is unconditional. Unconditional love has no limits, no limitations, and is given without expectation of return, and this is the love we must always strive to achieve. The closest relationship in which you may experience unconditional love may be from the divine, your parents, and if not either of these, perhaps from a pet. Most relationships in life are conditional in nature. Conditional relationships can be rewarding and mutually beneficial when the agreements for reciprocation are equitable, fair, and reasonable.

When you truly love someone, the expression of your love may ebb and flow, but the underlying intensity of love always remains. The foundation of true love continues even when conflicts or difficulties arise in relationships.

The nature of true love is pure, infinite, and one of the closest connections to the divine a human being can experience. Without this connection, we sever our relationship with others and with the divine spirit living within us and surrounding us at all times.

Every moment of love experienced is precious and never to be taken for granted. All too often people realize in hindsight how strong their love is for another or how wonderful it felt to be loved by that person. Learning to love and having the clarity to see your love in the present moment is the most intense and beautiful expression of love we can experience. For love to occur in the present moment, you must forgive the past, both yours and theirs, creating space now for your love to emerge. Become aware of whom you truly love in your life and who loves you, and then make sure you express your love to them regularly. The measure of how much we are able to love may be in the reflection of how much love we receive back from others.

54

Self-Love

Our most essential love is self-love; from self-love, all other love originates. At some point in your life, you must learn to truly love yourself, including your body, your mind, your life, and every action you have taken. Self-love is not some abstract idea or some behavior that is unachievable. Self-love is a process you engage in through the elements of self-respect, healthy boundaries, keeping personal commitments to yourself, living confidently from your values and beliefs, and your commitment to truth. Many people overlook the process of learning to love themselves, often suffering a lifetime of resulting negative consequences. Hell on earth may actually be a lifetime of never learning to love yourself. Nothing limits us more than self-hate, self-doubt, and the resulting diminished self-worth.

A truly loving person has great empathy and compassion for others, and for themselves in equal measure. Learning to love yourself and advocate for yourself is one of the first steps to self-actualizing an experience of life that is full and purposeful. If you are not the biggest advocate for yourself throughout your lifetime, who will be? Perhaps your parents? But when your parents are gone, who replaces them? You are to become your greatest advocate in this lifetime. Complete self-love and acceptance brings the awareness that you are your greatest advocate. From self-love, all love is reflected out from you into the world.

Self-forgiveness is foremost to learning to love oneself. We all make mistakes throughout life, but these must be forgiven and released at some point so we become free again to move forward joyfully and creatively, becoming all we can in this lifetime. When we judge ourselves harshly without forgiveness, this binds us to this judgment and condemnation forever. Without this forgiveness, we remain stuck in immoveable patterns of behavior that keep us in bondage to old ways of thinking and repetitive ways of behaving. Why would we ever condemn, berate, or not forgive ourselves?

Forgiving yourself and setting yourself free may be the most loving action you can take right now. So do it!

Self-love is the main component in the development of self-esteem. Self-esteem is comprised of the three elements of self-love, self-trust, and self-respect. Self-esteem occurs when you figure out what is right for you and then confidently make the right choices for yourself in any given moment. You align your actions with your desires and create a reality for yourself that builds trust in you and your unique abilities. Self-esteem develops from personal integrity as you continually evolve personal trust and personal respect.

Self-trust comes from living in congruence with your values and beliefs. What we believe and value must be reflected in every decision we make, every action we take, and every word we speak. You won't trust yourself if your behaviors and actions don't match the truth of your beliefs. When all of your outward behaviors match your inward beliefs, personal congruence and trust is established bringing peace to your whole being.

Personal respect comes from making and keeping commitments you've made to yourself and accomplishing the goals you set for yourself. The value and respect you have for yourself is a reflection of self-love. Everyone's needs can be considered, but your needs must be considered equally. Your intentions and desires must align with what you really want for yourself, and then be reflected in how you prioritize your needs and desires with the needs and desires of those around you. At some point you have to know what is right for you and take the steps to make your dreams, desires, and goals a reality.

Your self-love is also reflected in how you engage in relationship with others. When you love yourself, you are no longer willing to step into relationships that are hurtful, dysfunctional, or take away your energy through their drama or lack of contribution to your personal well-being. With self-love we become self-sufficient, complete and whole without total dependence on others for our peace, fulfillment, and happiness. Relationships enrich our lives, but we are not entirely dependent on them for our happiness, meaning and purpose. No one can fill the void created from a lack of self-love.

Loving yourself brings the awareness that you no longer need to subjugate your own needs, intentions, and desires to those of other people. On the other hand, self-love is not about excluding the needs of others and becoming self-centered. It is not about loving yourself more than others, but loving yourself equally with the ability to balance others' needs and desires with your own needs and desires. Too often we subjugate ourselves to other people by accepting hurtful or abusive behavior or by putting their needs above our needs. Loving yourself means standing up for yourself. You do not allow another person's ego, needs, or desires to diminish your right to your own reasonable needs and desires, which allows you to live life joyfully with peace and freedom.

Subjugation of our personal value should never exist in our relationships or in societal structures. Subjugation has been the cause for oppression and slavery throughout history. There are four times in our lives when our needs and desires are subjugated to the needs and desires of another: 1) when we are young children and our parents are teaching us the values and beliefs we need to navigate life; 2) when the agreed laws of a society must be followed for order and conduct to be maintained; 3) when we work for an employer and the management decides how we are to spend our time at work; and 4) when incarcerated in prison or jail. Beyond these, we have the right to freely express our fair and reasonable desires and not be subjugated to the needs or desires of others.

You love yourself by nurturing your body and soul through eating clean food, getting regular exercise, and performing those activities that bring you joy and spiritual connection. The more joy and connection you experience within yourself, the more you find the peace of personal fulfillment. Enjoyment of your body honors all of the sensations it presents to us to experience, and another expression of your love for yourself can be through the enjoyment of your body.

As your love for yourself grows, it expands outward toward others and all of life. Often it is through loving others that you learn to love yourself more fully. There is a realization that you can only love another person as much as you are capable of loving yourself. A self-loving and self-fulfilled being has an abundance of love and gifts to give to others. A person who does not love, honor, or respect themselves cannot love, honor, and respect others, and has no gifts of abundance to share.

It may take a lifetime to fully experience the gifts of self-love, but it is never too late to begin the healing process provided to us through self-love: a process that continually nurtures you throughout your life, as your ability for self-love and love of others is infinitely possible in both its expression and capacity.

Romantic Love

To love truly and to be truly loved can be one of life's greatest gifts. Romantic love can happen in many ways. It can be instantaneous, evolve gradually over time, or appear unexpectedly. Love often occurs when we least expect it or are not even looking for it. For most, a deeply loving relationship is a gradual process of learning to love each other by being together and having shared experiences over time.

The best romantic partners are usually best friends, for the familiarity of friendship and companionship builds a solid foundation upon which to base a romantic relationship. Added to the friendship are the additional elements of attraction, passion, sexual desire, and sexual intimacy, allowing for other expressions of our love. The sexual act of union between two physical bodies can be one of the deepest expressions of love we can share.

The love we feel for our partners or spouses may exceed all other loves. Being told "I love you" is a powerful affirmation for any relationship. Writing "I love you" to someone can be an even more powerful affirmation, for it holds permanence in written form. The most affirming love is to show a person your love for them through actions each day, for through the cumulative effect of all of our words and actions we truly express our love for another.

Unrequited love occurs when the love felt for another is not returned in kind, not felt to the same level, or not willingly received. While unrequited love can be painful and feel like rejection, we can be comforted in knowing we do not want to force love or pursue a love not willingly returned to us. You cannot sacrifice your own peace and happiness for the promise of love that will not happen. Unrequited love does not always have to end a relationship, but it may require a step back to a level of intimacy mutually agreeable to both people involved.

When there is a disparity in the amount of money earned or the money held by either person in a romantic relationship, the one with the greater money or assets is not necessarily entitled to more weight when it comes to the decisions that affect both people. There are other currencies in relationships not based on money including our love, energy, care, support, sharing, and time together which should account for contribution to the relationship as well. Over time these softer currencies should weigh in to the relational equation with just as much consideration as money weighs in.

When we are younger, we may not value love and may take it for granted when it appears. As we grow older, we may cherish and value the love we have known and feel regret for the love we let slip away. Always give love every possible consideration and cherish love when it looks your way.

When you do find true love, handle it with all the delicate care and attention it deserves. Love needs regular care and attention to keep it nurtured, cared for, and received in kind. Love grows when it receives this nurturing. When we love, we also want love in return, but must surrender and trust that love has its own timing and will be returned to us in one form or another. When true love shows up, regard it with all the respect and loving attention it deserves.

When we have been hurt or rejected, it can be easy to become jaded and to no longer believe in love, but remaining open to love allows us to receive it when it appears. The heart may be broken many times, and from this pain a belief can arise that love does not exist, is perceived as lost, unrequited, or forgotten. However, love *does* exist, is always willing and available, and can show up anytime, anywhere, when you least expect it, only asking that we be open to receive it.

Non-Romantic Love

Your ability to love is all that matters in this lifetime. We often overlook how love shows up for us in all of our connections. Love can also show up in our non-romantic relationships including friendships and family, and even some casual acquaintances. Most of us learned how to love from our parents through how they expressed their love for one another and for us, even if their patterns of behavior were not always loving or based on loving behaviors. If they bought gifts to express their love, then we might expect gifts or gift giving as the expression of love. If one parent was constantly rescuing the other parent, then we may equate rescuing behavior as love. If they argued and then made up, we might require disagreement or arguments with others and the corresponding resolution in order to feel loved. With more awareness of how we learned to love, we can recognize those patterns that are not necessarily loving but rather learned behavior patterns mistaken for love.

Investigating how your expressions of love might be linked to your family of origin serves to help us understand how to love. Such study can be a doorway to understanding if these expressions are *truly* loving, or if they are actually unhealthy and dysfunctional patterns we learned as coping mechanisms in childhood.

While our family can include some of the most loving relationships we experience in a lifetime, our parents and siblings can also be the people in our lives who push our limits and test our boundaries the most. They can also evolve to be some of our healthiest and most loving *Adult* relationships, if allowed. Our parents and siblings may know better than anyone else how to stir us into motion or stir up our emotions. When motivated by love, family can be our greatest advocate to get us moving forward toward needed change.

Our love cannot enable blindness to unhealthy or dysfunctional behavior with family or friends. Family is often given special rights or leniency to abuse us or treat us in unloving and unkind ways *just because they are our family*. Even when their actions, words, or behaviors are hurtful or destructive, we often grant family members much more leniency than we would other people. Not even family gets to make excuses for un-*Adult* behavior, but we may be more willing to forgive family. Healthy families engage as loving *Adults* based on the same healthy relationship principals of intimacy, honesty, reciprocity, trust, and respect. Setting clear boundaries with a family member who cannot engage as an *Adult* may be the most loving action we can make for ourselves and for them.

Friendships, or those relationships without the elements of romance and sexual desire, can be some of the most loving relationships we sustain over a lifetime. While platonic love may not have the depth of romantic love, a breadth of loving friendships is equally important. The diversity and sheer number of these relationships in our lifetime brings richness to our lives, and for some may be the only connections in which true love is experienced. We often forget that while we have families we are born into and may love dearly, as adults our friends may also become our chosen family, bringing lasting love and meaning to our lives. Giving these relationships the care, love, and respect they deserve continually nurtures the riches that friendships can return to us.

Beyond our friends and family, we can aspire to a more universal love, a love extending outward to all beings on this planet. Universal love dawns in our awareness when we realize the true connectivity we have to everything and to all beings. Love for yourself and for others can grow and open to an experience of universal love for all life. Love allows for the possibility of a world in which every being finds their rightful place in the grand connectivity of all of existence.

With universal love comes great compassion and empathy for all of life and this planet on which we live together. Acceptance and inclusion are expressions of love, whereas judgmentalism, exclusion, and apathy represent unloving behaviors. Approach anything you don't understand with love and acceptance, not with judgment and separation. As we experience the depths of joy and sorrow life offers, we also feel connected with the bliss and pathos of all life forms. Our personal understanding of human suffering and the perceived tragedy of existence teach us to honor everyone and everything in our lives with a deep respect and wonder. When all is considered and viewed in relationship to everything else, love may ultimately be all that matters and the purest expression of existence. Always extend love, and you will always be loved.

Empathy

As you love yourself, love naturally extends outwards and expresses itself through you as empathy toward others. Empathy is an emotion that reflects our ability to step outside of ourselves and into another's life situation. From this perspective, we can consciously become attuned to what another person may be feeling, thinking, or experiencing. Empathy opens us up to inquisitiveness. Inquisitiveness brings us to a greater understanding of other people and ourselves. Through empathy we are able to have a better understanding of others and their behaviors. Developing empathy occurs when you seek to understand another's place of vulnerability or hardship. From this understanding, actions can be taken to assist that person in supportive ways, such as listening to their feelings, helping if possible, or simply showing up with your presence and support during difficult times.

To cultivate empathy with another person, you can ask yourself, *How would I want to be treated in this situation?* or *What would it feel like to go through what this person is going through?* When we become aware of our true connection to everything and everyone, our empathy allows us to see the joy, the pathos, the struggles, and the successes of every human we encounter.

The opposite of empathy is unfeeling and indifference. Unfeeling and indifference lead to inaction, and inaction is a clear sign we are disconnected from our inner divine being and the divine connecting us to everything and everyone. Doing nothing or saying nothing when someone is suffering or in need represents unfeeling. Engaged with life we are empathetic; disconnected from life we are insensitive or unfeeling. Empathy is the expression of the heart. Insensitive is the expression of the ego. We can become overly empathetic through attachment, or completely disengaged through avoidance. Our goal as *Adults* is to continually reconnect with life and ourselves through our expression of empathy, for this leads to balance and equanimity with other living beings and the world around us.

Out of empathy arises awareness of how our thoughts, words, actions, or inactions affect other people. Our empathy for others and how we are able to express empathy grows as we look at the outcomes or effects of our behavior on others over time. We often find that empathy is not about just having feelings of pity or sorrow, but also involves action to help or console another. Pity, if it does not come from a place of love with loving actions, is a condolence with no value to the person being pitied.

Empathy for others teaches us to see the world and other people from different perspectives. When we have a strong emotional capacity for empathy, we are sensitive to see clearly what action could be taken to help another, if any. Sometimes what we don't do matters most or can be more revealing. Empathy can also lead to insight on how to resolve some of the world's larger problems by using our knowledge to help others who are less fortunate or need our assistance.

Our empathy can lead us to take action in emergency situations or in situations in which we observe unfair or cruel behavior by others and we step in to assist. While empathy may not always lead to action, it can at least give us a better understanding of others or their life circumstances.

The difference between empathy and rescuing behavior can be a fine line. Empathy becomes *rescuing behavior* when we take on another's hurt or hardship as our personal emotional suffering, or actually step in and try to fix another's problem when our help is unwanted, when we cannot fix it, or they are capable of fixing it for themselves. Stay vigilant to see that empathy does not lead to rescuing behavior or the taking on or wallowing in the problems and emotional burdens of others. Your gifts of abundance come from integrating wholeness, not from fueling another's perceived lack. Empathy is not about making someone else's hardship about you by over-personalizing the person's suffering or difficulties. The most loving gift you can give to someone who is working through problems, hardships, or difficult times is to provide your presence, comfort, and offer of support, as well as advice or guidance when asked. Sometimes simply sending a prayer of well-being that the highest good will unfold in the person's time of need can be a powerful form of support. However, prayer combined with actions show one's truer intention of support.

Another aspect of empathy is supporting another in their wishes and dreams, even if these do not align with your own needs, values, or aspirations for them. Selflessness may be the extreme expression of empathy, in which giving for the greater good or betterment of another's needs exceeds one's own personal needs or desires. A person who truly loves or cares for you wants your happiness and supports your wishes and desires based on this love for you. The person does not just support those wishes or desires that meet their needs only, but rather supports what you want for yourself, especially that which brings you happiness. If a person is more interested in supporting only those desires or intents that meet primarily their needs, this is not love, but comes from a self-centered state that is not truly empathetic to your needs and desires.

Be happy for other people's successes, even when your life is not going well. The last thing you want for yourself is someone jealous and unhappy because of your happiness or success. Likewise, extend your energy generously by being happy for others when they experience happiness and success.

Mothers naturally have great empathy because they have always had to consider the needs of their children, often before their own. The process of carrying a child for nine months and then going through childbirth brings joy, sacrifice, and great pain. The innate empathy mothers feel for their children and others may come from the experience of connection to the child within, and the process of childbirth into a world of uncertainty. The process of such immense personal pain also brings forth the joy of new life into the world, a true miracle of creation, needing all of the love and protection we can provide. Our mothers, childbirth and their maternal energy can teach us all more empathy.

We can incorporate a practice of empathy into our life daily by being more mindful in our interactions with those we know, and with complete strangers. Before you impose your expectations and demands that your needs be met by someone in your life, stop and take the life circumstances of others into consideration and adjust your needs or expectations accordingly. Life is not easy for any of us, and becoming empathetic to other people's circumstances is another way in which we can show love for them. The simplest acts of unexpected consideration can penetrate our hearts the deepest.

The level of awareness a person achieves may best be reflected in one's empathy for others, awareness of the world, and how one's words, actions, and behaviors affect others. Our words and how we use them become especially important. Saying what we think or what we feel with no filters for how our words affect other people shows a lack of empathy for others and a lower level of awareness. Good filters are knowing what is appropriate, and what is inappropriate to say in a given context of audience and the level of intimacy shared.

Whatever harm you cause to another being, you also cause to yourself, so always be mindful of your intent for the highest good of all involved. Compassion is the natural outflow of our capacity for empathy. A regular practice of compassion and empathy can heal each of us individually, and collectively the world. Developing empathy and compassion is the work of a lifetime, but the rewards along the way are many, both large and small.

CHAPTER FIVE

Intimacy

W hy today, with all of the ways we have to communicate, do we feel disconnected from one another? Why do some relationships seem more meaningful than others? Has technology brought us closer connections, or created more distance? To answer these questions and more, we have to look at *intimacy* and how we develop and sustain meaningful connections in our lives through intimacy.

The experience of separation from ourselves and from each other is the reason we desire more intimate relationships. There is a direct correlation between the amount of intimacy we have with others and our feelings of belonging and connection. It is not about how many people we surround ourselves with, but rather how much intimacy we experience in our current relationships. Intimacy is the expression of the gravitational force between people that attracts them. Without intimacy we remain separate or at its worst, repelled.

Intimacy exists when you make yourself emotionally available through the communication of your vulnerability and honesty. While life is rich with different experiences, intimacy and intimate conversation are the most rewarding experiences we can have. Why? Because we feel alive and that we belong through the connections we establish and maintain with others. Without intimacy, our relationships can feel empty, disconnected, and meaningless. Consequently, we often attempt to fill the void created by a lack of intimacy with activities and distractions such as more work, alcohol, drugs, distractions, or other addictions. Yet the true connection we yearn for in ourselves and with others only comes through an increased capacity for intimate relationships. This connection cannot be filled through distractions or addictions.

Intimacy is expressed through our communications, our shared activities, and behaviors that bring us into deeper connection with others. Intimacy is not just the expression of love or affection between romantic partners. Intimacy exists throughout all of our relationships to varying degrees. The deeper connection of intimacy builds a foundation and context from which any relationship can evolve. While love is the fiber that connects us, intimacy is the strength in those fibers.

The information engines we see and hear around us every day make us feel separate by projecting their definition of what is beautiful, smart, and successful, rather than showing how we are all connected on this planet through our shared humanity and how each individual contributes their own unique gifts. The images we are bombarded with through advertising and media often separate us rather than bring us together in meaningful connections we all desire. We put ourselves in cars, cubicles, and walled off offices for large amounts of time each day, further increasing our feelings of isolation. What most of us feel on a regular basis is the human desire to connect with and be accepted by other humans. The good news is the connection and acceptance we find missing from society today can be reestablished through the development of deeper intimacy in our relationships.

Intimacy can take many forms and expressions, depending on the type of relationship involved. A connection with another person can be emotional in nature or it can be physical, such as a reassuring hug or sexual contact with a romantic partner. Many people avoid human touch and misinterpret touching or hugging as something sexual, which of course is not always the case. As *Adults*, we need the closeness of other people through touch on a daily basis, but sadly, many adults miss this basic nourishment of being touched by another human being.

Emotional intimacy occurs when two or more people feel safe enough to share their most honest thoughts or feelings, or to participate in intimate behaviors that are welcoming and open. Intimacy provides a shared space where people can be heard, valued, and honored for the depth of their vulnerability. Emotional intimacy is born out of vulnerability and the ability to share one's honest feelings. Speaking the truth and being vulnerable allows us to know one another on deeper and more satisfying levels.

Permission is required for the development of intimacy. A relationship can develop greater trust and intimacy when we give one another permission to be completely honest and express our innermost feelings, our joys, our sorrows, and our fears. As permission for honesty and vulnerability increases, deeper intimacy develops. When we judge, restrict, limit, censor or cannot be honest then intimacy suffers or is ultimately not possible. Honesty and vulnerability are refreshing in both their directness and authenticity when we become comfortable using them and acclimated to receiving them.

The unfolding of intimacy between two people requires giving the connection time and space to develop. No one can understand the level of intimacy that develops between two people except the two people involved in an intimate relationship. This is the nature of intimacy and intimate relationships: each connection is a unique intimate relationship not interdependent on other relationships.

Beyond the critical elements of honesty, trust, permission, and the willingness to be vulnerable, intimacy is developed through the care and priority of importance we give to a relationship. Most of us have an inner circle consisting of our most intimate relationships. Other relationships— with varying degrees of intimacy—fall outside of this circle. All relationships must add intimate value to our lives for the connection to remain sustainable in any meaningful way.

The opposite of intimacy is superficiality. Superficiality occurs when there are limited amounts of truth and vulnerability exchanged. Superficiality in relationships leads to feelings of complete disconnectedness. If we do not have intimacy with others or personal intimacy with ourselves, we feel lost, alone, and disconnected. Engaging in intimacy and intimate conversations are the most rewarding human experiences we can have. Without intimacy, relationships quickly become superficial and meaningless.

Vulnerability

Most people are afraid of being truthful, because being truthful about yourself or your feelings renders one extremely vulnerable. Being vulnerable can be perceived as weak, whereas the opposite is actually true. People who are vulnerable and truthful are the strongest and most courageous people you will encounter. The ability to be authentic and vulnerable[3] allows you and your relationships to experience life with other humans in a rich and deeply rewarding way. Personal intimacy must first be established so that we can connect to our honest feelings and vulnerability, and are then able to express these through words and behaviors outwardly to others.

For an intimate relationship to develop, both people must be willing to let down their defenses, insecurities, and fears and share in their vulnerability. If the vulnerability and openness to intimacy is only coming from one person or feels one sided or unequal, then eventually the person being intimate senses this inequality and will pull back their intimacy to a level of intimacy the other person is capable of giving or receiving.

Fear of intimacy and fear of vulnerability go hand in hand. People often fear intimacy because intimacy means vulnerability, which means they may have to feel painful feelings they have worked hard to suppress. There is always the potential to feel pain when we expose our innermost feelings, but the potential benefits and the possibility of healing these painful places far outweigh the negative consequences. It is often in the sharing of our deepest vulnerabilities that we become healed and set completely free. Any fear of

---

[3] The definition of vulnerable used here is in the context of one's ability to express their innermost feelings, which is related, but different from the Vulnerable position in the Healthy Triangle, where it is indicative of a person in a position of Vulnerability.

intimacy can be eliminated when we gradually develop shared trust together and gradually learn to be comfortable in being vulnerable.

It takes courage to share our intimate thoughts and feelings, as sometimes we are afraid others will reject us if they truly know us. We fear we might be judged or will expose ourselves to some kind of hurt from others. However, being intimate also means the creation of a safe space in which we give each other permission to discuss difficult or emotionally charged topics without judgement or limitation. Trust is established through mutual permission given to express deeper intimacy.

The rewards of intimacy far outweigh the negatives of potential rejection. You cannot be intimate without being honest. You cannot be honest without being vulnerable. The depth of truth and vulnerability you are willing to share determines the depth of intimacy you experience. Personal intimacy develops by being honest with yourself about what you are thinking and feeling and then giving yourself the permission to be who you are and where you are in this moment.

How Do We Develop Intimacy?

We all experience varying degrees of intimacy, but we must develop personal intimacy with ourselves before we can develop deeper intimacy with others. Personal intimacy is developed through the ability to consciously observe our thoughts and feelings, and how they are interrelated. Getting clear on how our emotions affect our thoughts and how our thoughts affect our emotions helps to develop an emotional vocabulary that comes closer to a complete expression of our true selves. This deeper level of communication opens the door for more personal intimacy and meaningful connections with other beings.

Personal intimacy must first be established with ourselves before we can engage intimately with others. We develop personal intimacy by connecting to our innermost honest feelings and raw vulnerability. From observation of our feelings and vulnerability we then develop an emotional, physical, and verbal vocabulary to express these, first to ourselves, and with more experience, outwardly to others.

Most people are not in touch with what they are feeling, because they do not take the time to stop and observe their emotions or to become conscious of the different energetic responses occurring in their bodies. What we think is only part of having an experience. When we observe what we feel, we bring our emotions into the experience. When we add the observation of energy sensations throughout our body, we bring forth awareness of our visceral response to an experience. When we add collectively what we think, feel, and sense, these responses bring us closer to the truth of an experience. There must be a balance established between the thinking mind and the feeling heart. Too much thinking can cause you to over analyze every situation or experience that arises. Too much feeling can have you responding and acting on every emotion that arises. Of these three, leading with our feelings and then seeing what thoughts and sensations arise may serve us best.

However, once you become practiced at stopping and observing your thoughts, feelings, and senses in the present moment, being too direct and honest in your communication can come across as harsh or abrasive. You do not have to state verbally everything you think, feel, and sense. Your message becomes stronger when there is awareness of the timing for what is said, as well as sensitivity to the best possible way to express your intention and meaning. Learning to filter our thoughts, feelings and senses for what is most appropriate is an ongoing process dependent upon varying circumstances and audiences.

Becoming aware of our thoughts, feelings and senses cultivates a personal intimacy with our inner selves. We all have conversations with ourselves, experience sensations and feel emotions constantly. Through the process of observing ourselves, we begin to gain clarity about what feels right and becomes a "yes" inside and what feels wrong and becomes a "no." Through this process, we start to discover for ourselves, in the present moment, what we are actually feeling, thinking, sensing, desiring, and what we cherish, how we attach, how we avoid, and many more aspects of our true self. The more personal intimacy you develop with yourself, the better you are at communication and the more compassionately you are able to show up intimately for others.

People who lack the skills of intimacy find it uncomfortable to talk about what they are feeling, particularly in the case of earlier generations of men that were not encouraged to express their feelings or to be vulnerable. For most men, emotional vulnerability was seen as a sign of weakness. All too often little girls were given permission to be vulnerable, cry and express their feelings, while little boys were told not to cry, to be strong, to "be a little man," and given the message it was not "masculine" to express their inner feelings or emotions. For boys to feel or express their emotions, or to cry, was perceived as weak, while girls were given full permission to do so. This taught generations of little boys to shut down or repress their feelings to a large degree and gave a clear message that they were not to feel. Furthermore, whereas boys were allowed to express anger and be competitive, girls were taught to repress their anger and not be as competitive. Encouraging children to experience the full range of feelings and sensations and then encouraging them to verbalize these will help future generations express themselves intimately.

Emotional vulnerability is the more truthful state of humans, and repressing or allowing our thoughts to supersede our feelings has led to disconnection from ourselves and discouragement from forming connections with others. The true strength of any individual comes when one is in touch with their feelings and can be vulnerable and honest enough to express those feelings with another person. Diminishing or negating any of this prevents us from intimacy and emotional honesty within ourselves and with others.

Intimacy is also developed through the act of *confidentiality*, which is the ability to keep intimate conversations private. When you hold the sharing of another's thoughts and feelings as private and confidential, a sacred trust develops in which the energy of intimacy can deepen between the two of you. Another benefit of confidentiality is the level of personal integrity it takes to hold another's confidence which creates a deeper relationship of intimacy within yourself. You learn that not only are you trustworthy with others, but that you can also trust yourself.

No matter what generation, no matter what age, it is never too late, or too early, to begin the process of developing personal intimacy and intimate connections with others. If you are just beginning to understand intimacy skills and to have intimate interactions, start by surrounding yourself with people with whom you are given permission and feel comfortable to be more honest and more vulnerable. Any relationship that gives us full permission to be who we are and to express our innermost thoughts and feelings will bring the rewards of lasting intimacy.

The Elements of Intimate Conversations

A conversation that is honest, vulnerable and shares ideas and feelings can be the most rewarding experience you can have as a human being. An intimate conversation not only involves sharing your thoughts but also your feelings, your emotions, your space, and your time.

Intimacy requires that we engage without being distracted by other people, taking other phone calls, reading texts, or even being preoccupied with your own thoughts about what you will say or do next. Staying physically, mentally and emotionally present during an entire conversation or interaction allows intimacy to unfold. When you show up and are fully present in the moments together, there is a felt sense of intimacy between both people in the relationship. Similarly, if you are distracted and not present, the other person will feel distance. Our most intimate connections occur in the physical presence of others, not through cell phones, texts, emails or social media. The act of showing up and being present for another can be one of the most intimate and respectful acts you can give.

An intimate conversation has the following elements:

1. Permission is granted to express any true thoughts, feelings, and senses that arise, without limitation, labeling, or judgment.

2. Both people share a willingness to be vulnerable and openly express their vulnerability.

3. There is a natural flow to the conversation through a reciprocal back and forth, with no one person dominating the interaction, and each is allowed to express his/herself uninterrupted.

4. The energy of openness and honesty permeates the conversation, allowing a mutual trust and feeling of intimacy to be developed over time.

5. There is an agreement of confidentiality, spoken or unspoken, about the thoughts, feelings, or emotions being shared.

6. For intimacy to unfold, each person must be congruent and authentic both in speech and body language.

7. Both people have equal opportunity to speak and both engage actively to listen.

Notice the elements above require equal participation by both parties. This act of *mutual* engagement is important, because intimacy can only develop when there is complete presence and willingness from all involved. If a person relates to you only what he or she does or thinks, and not what is felt, the ensuing conversations are not as meaningful, interesting, or intimate. Feelings must be part of the shared interaction, even if they are simply feelings about activities or experiences that are occurring, have occurred, or will occur.

Listening is the most important skill we can improve as we strive to develop deeper intimate relationships. Listening to what another is thinking and feeling is as important as sharing your own thoughts and feelings. Everyone wants their time to be listened to and be heard. We feel valued when what we have said is heard, acknowledged, and understood. If we are misunderstood, censored, or not heard, then we do not feel valued. For any relationship to continue to grow, particularly a romantic relationship, each person must develop the ability to listen effectively to the other, with full comprehension and full understanding of what is actually being said.

After years of knowing someone or living together, you may think you know how someone thinks and feels or how they will react to any given situation. This is actually a form of arrogance that can erode the potential for intimacy because it ignores the fact that we are all constantly changing. How we respond to any given situation can change over time. This perceived familiarity limits our ability to experience deeper intimacy, rather than enhancing it. Listening, without projecting how you might respond or what you think they might feel or experience, allows you to come closer to deeper understanding. We can never truly know another person, but active listening can heighten our determination to uncover the mystery.

Active listening is the ability to engage in an interaction with genuine interest, as expressed through the questions you ask and the physical cues you display outwardly. Questions and physical cues demonstrate you are listening and understand the subtler meanings and emotions being communicated. You might ask, "How did that make you feel?" or "Can you tell me more about what you mean by _____?" Asking questions shows you are interested in what's being shared. When an answer is provided and received with genuine interest, additional understanding is reached. Questions alone do not provide more intimacy; our genuine interest in hearing the other person's answer and a clear understanding of what is said brings us into more intimacy.

Our body language also shows we are open to intimacy when we are comfortable, relaxed, and receptive. Active listening includes physical components such as eye contact during the interaction, positioning oneself physically close enough to hear what is being said, and then speaking at a volume that can be heard clearly. Nodding the head and providing other physical cues of acknowledgement or agreement can also show that you are present and engaged in the conversation.

Asking people what they think is not as intimate as asking them what they feel. Similarly, asking, "How are you doing?" does not lead to intimate conversation as quickly as asking, "What are you feeling?"

Additionally, if conversations are limited to the obvious, then it doesn't feel like a meaningful dialogue has transpired. What is mundane or obvious to both does not always make interesting intimate conversations. Authentic conversation usually includes an infusion of honest feelings until a deeper level of understanding has occurred in the interaction. Sometimes this kind of truthful and authentic communication allows for an opening wherein one person's vulnerability provides a space for the other person to become more vulnerable and open.

Intimacy also means having the conviction to express your personal feelings even when they may not be agreed with or accepted by the other party. Sometimes a meaningful conversation includes expressing new views and ideas differing from another person's views. If both parties continually allow permission for the discussion to flow without attachment to their opinions or beliefs, then the conversation can continue to unfold and become a meaningful dialogue during which deeper understanding and meaning are achieved. Healthy conversations are mostly dialogues, with occasional monologues.

When an intimate conversation centers on problems or difficult situations, determine if you are being asked just to listen and hear what is being presented, or if you are being asked to provide feedback. Sometimes people only want to express their feelings with someone or share their difficult life experiences and are not asking for feedback. If there is ever uncertainty about what a person is wanting from you, when they finish speaking you can ask, "Do you want to hear my thoughts or feedback, or would you rather I just listen?" And then you honor their response.

Venting is the act of relaying feelings, sometimes negative, about another person or situation that are emotionally charged, difficult, or uncomfortable. Venting is fine in the larger context of many intimate conversations. However, a person who constantly vents their frustrations is not usually looking for an intimate conversation, but rather just wants to unload their emotional charge onto another. We all vent our frustrations from time to time, but too much venting can become one-sided, obstructing intimate interaction between the people involved and requiring too much of the time and energy needed to sustain a mutually intimate relationship.

Through intimacy, we can understand the diversity of the people in our lives and their approach to life. Our differences are the spice of life and make our interactions with others interesting. Intimate conversation creates a space where we can begin to understand the diversity of humans, their differences, and their experiences. Through engaging with others in an open, intimate, and nonjudgmental manner, we can learn more about ourselves and discover other ways of approaching life both individually and culturally.

What Are Intimate Behaviors?

Behaviors expressing intimacy include eye contact, active listening, and physical acts such as hugging, patting someone on the back, or a gentle touch. Other intimate behaviors might include written notes, cards, letters, or emails expressing fondness. Just the simple act of calling someone to catch up on what's new shows we care and desire an intimate connection. A friend who has just lost a loved one may want you to hug them, or hold them. You may hug or kiss a friend or family member on the cheek when you greet them. Obviously, in romantic relationships, intimate behavior can include holding another person, passionate kisses, or sexual intimacy.

In today's society there can be a fine line between showing affection through intimate behavior, and what is socially acceptable based on the type of relationship. Getting clear on what the intentions are behind the affection and the social context can be helpful. Occasionally physical acts of affection may be mistaken for flirting or sexual advance, when in reality these are just kind and loving behaviors. If there is any ambiguity, then set clear verbal boundaries, or get clarification of the other's intentions.

Time is an essential element of intimacy, because with each intimate encounter with another person, trust and intimacy deepen. As the trust grows so does vulnerability, as each person feels safer to share their innermost personal feelings. If betrayal of trust occurs at any point, then both parties can become more guarded in what is said and shared, and it may take time to get back to a deeper level of trust and intimacy.

Space is also required for intimate relationships. For friends, this may mean some occasional time together in person for a shared experience. For more romantic relationships, a combination of time and space alone—not in the presence of others—is needed. Both parties are responsible for taking care of the relationship by cultivating intimate conversations and intimate moments together, discussing and finding solutions to obstacles in the relationship, and taking care of each other's needs. Without regular intervals of time spent together and the privacy needed to nurture and reaffirm a relationship, most relationships eventually fall apart, and people move on in search of more intimate connections.

Authentic relationships and intimate interactions with others become more desired as you begin to reap the rewards of real connections and a felt sense of belonging. Consequently, the *quality* of intimate and honest communication with others becomes a priority in your life and in your intimate relationships.

Intimacy in Groups

Intimacy can occur between groups of more than two people; however, in a group situation of three or more people, the level of intimacy shared defaults to the level of the person with the least amount of intimacy skills. People in a group setting find themselves stepping back to adjust their level of intimacy accordingly, out of respect and kindness, so no one feels left out of the intimate interaction. If a person is unable or unwilling to share their feelings and engage in intimacy, then over time the friendship or relationship remains at superficial or casual level lacking the deeper communication and intimacy to take it further.

In large groups, if enough people are engaged intimately, those who do not or cannot engage intimately gradually become quiet or leave the gathering. Deeper intimacy can be uncomfortable for those who are not experienced in intimacy. Also, you may find that when people cannot engage in intimacy, they may stand by and observe the intimate interaction without participating. In the meantime, being observed by someone not participating at the same level of intimacy eventually becomes uncomfortable for the people who are engaged intimately. Our continual encouragement of those less intimate to step into more intimacy brings us closer to the connections we all desire.

People who are not capable of intimacy are often unaware that they actually want more intimacy in their lives. Instead of learning additional intimacy skills, they may try to compensate for lack of intimacy by wanting to spend extraneous time distracted with work or with other people who are superficial. Intimacy is about both the quality and quantity of time. People who don't know how to engage in intimacy may try to substitute time for intimacy and ask for more quantity of time spent together to compensate for their unconscious need for deeper intimacy. They may also become jealous of other intimate relationships around them because of their own lack of intimacy skills and inability to engage intimately.

Certain intimate behaviors do not need any expression in mixed company. For example, if two people are in a romantic intimate relationship, and living with a third person, it is appropriate to express physical intimacy behind closed doors and not in the company of others. Displays of affection that lead to passionate kissing or fondling in the presence of others are inappropriate and make others feel uncomfortable.

A group situation in which everyone is engaged intimately can be a dynamic setting nurturing everyone present. In any group gathering, the needs of the individual must be balanced with the overall needs of the group. As we all learn more intimacy skills, our interactions with others and with groups change over time. Those unwilling or incapable of sharing intimacy will want to raise their awareness of intimacy to engage in the human connection that strengthens the fiber of our existence...*Intimacy*!

Humor, Jokes, and Banter

Humor may be one of the best personality traits we can possess and share with others. Humor allows us to experience views of life that are lighter, more joyful, and may allow us to laugh at our life situations and hopefully even at ourselves. Without humor, life can become ponderous and serious. Laughter may be our best medicine in difficult times, such as when we need healing or shifting of our energy to see life from a different perspective.

While sarcasm, joking, and banter can bring entertainment to our relationships, they can also reduce intimacy or be used as a way to avoid intimacy. Continual use of sarcasm becomes hard to tolerate and can start to create more distance in relationships. Similarly, demeaning or derogatory comments cloaked as jokes or banter can cause us to feel devalued and reduce our self-esteem. Those who degrade others often use this to make up for their own lack of self-esteem, or inability to engage intimately.

Jokes are fine when they are about innocuous topics, but can be hurtful when the content or intent is at the expense of others. The basis for all humor is truth. When jokes or banter have elements of truth that are hurtful to others or groups of people, then these may actually be passive aggressive ways a person chooses to express their hurt, judgment, or unresolved issues in relationship to others. This type of joking and banter has the effect of alienating and reducing the trust and respect of the targeted person. Words used to address or describe someone that are negative in connotation are best

81

not used even jokingly, as the true meaning of the words still resonates even when spoken jokingly.

Humor at the expense of someone else's feelings can also be a coping mechanism to avoid discussing a difficult topic. Such situations should be addressed each time they arise, because no one's pain or suffering should be the brunt of someone else's jokes or banter.

Joking and banter can become excessive, leaving no real truth exchanged as the basis for honest communication in the relationship. While humor is always welcome, it must be balanced with the addition of sincerity and truth.

Whenever you are joking, bantering, or even using sarcasm, consider your audience. What we think is funny is not necessarily what someone else will find funny. There must be sensitivity to know when humor will entertain and when it might potentially offend others. It is better to err on the side of not telling certain jokes if there is risk of offending others. We really do not always know if another person thinks as we do, shares our beliefs, or agrees with our notion of what is humorous. Some of the more common categories of offensive jokes and banter that are best avoided in mixed company include sexuality, age, gender specific issues, disability, body weight, race, death, disease, or illness.

Healthy sharing of laughter with others and connecting through humor can be one of life's greatest pleasures. Laughter provides a "music to the ears" experience that is contagious. When we hear someone laughing, we want to laugh back and share in the experience. Happiness is our natural state, and humor can express our happiness. Finding humor that is never at the expense of others serves to enhance the good times and lessen the burden of difficult times.

Intimacy and Conflicts

Conflicts create the opportunity to build more intimacy. When each person is willing to take personal responsibility for their part in the conflict or misunderstanding, and both can come together with a clear intention for resolving the conflict, an opportunity for the development of deeper intimacy exists. Through conflict, we can come to understand a person more completely, their boundaries, what motivates them, attracts, repels, triggers, and what brings peace. Looking at conflicts as a means to greater personal and interpersonal knowledge can serve as a fertile ground to clear obstacles and bring us closer together. We tend to gravitate naturally to relationships with those who approach the world and conflicts in much the same manner as we do.

Personal responsibility for each person's part in a conflict is critical. The two most healing words on the planet are "I'm sorry," and while using these words to clear up problems or misunderstandings doesn't cost a thing, it can heal a lot. Saying "I'm sorry" versus saying "I apologize" are different. The former represents a more heartfelt apology expressing empathy, while the latter comes across as more general in nature. It either case, personal admission of the offending behavior associated with the apology is always more substantial. When personal responsibility is not stated or implied with the apology given, the sincerity of the person apologizing may not be believable.

What can be helpful in any conflict is beginning from the awareness that the ego wants to protect its beliefs and not be wrong. You become vulnerable when you admit you are wrong and perform the exact opposite of how the ego wants you to respond. Egoic pride can stand in the way of admitting we are wrong or conceding our vulnerability. Pride can end relationships if the need to be *right* is not supplanted with the need to be *fair*. Admitting our mistakes is a healthy *Adult* behavior that shows we are in balance within ourselves. Humility can bring us back into harmony and balance with others by providing the means for trust. Non-admission or covering of our mistakes leads only to more distrust.

Saying "I'm sorry" also demonstrates to the other person and to yourself the maturity to accept responsibility for your actions, even when they are not always right. "I'm sorry" also shows the other person that you respect and care enough and are willing to offer personal responsibility to clear the air so the relationship can move forward. If a conflict occurs in front of other people, then the apology is best done in front of the people involved so everyone is witness to the apology and feels the resolution to the conflict.

Be wary of the person who has mastered the words "I'm sorry" to get out of repeated bad behavior or to avoid discussing what went wrong. If "I'm sorry" is said too often it comes to have less meaning or no meaning at all.

If "I'm sorry" is not apology enough, then what statement or action would make amends? Are amends even possible? It is important to acknowledge an apology when it is received. If an apology is ignored or there is movement forward without acknowledgment, the apology is probably not accepted and feelings of resentment may remain. When we continue to hold on to unfulfilled expectations, this causes resentment. What serves us best when we feel resentful is to let go of our expectations and decide what different choices we would make to avoid conflicts, what boundaries to set in the future, or what expectations we can reset or omit.

An apology received cannot be used to hold you or others indebted. This occurs when a person apologizes and the individual receiving the apology doesn't accept it or accepts it conditionally. This type of behavior stops the healing process that began with the apology, and if the apology is used against them or used to subjugate them, the individual who experiences these conditional apologies is less likely to apologize in the future.

Conflicts in personal intimate relationships are always personal and best not aired publicly. Everyone becomes uncomfortable around a couple having problems, especially when we are forced to witness their conflicts or resulting bickering publicly. As an observer in this, you have the right to ask them to

84

engage in their conflicted behavior when they are alone or at least, not in your presence.

In general and whenever possible, conflicts are best kept private between the people engaged in the conflict. When either party engages other people to garner support for their individual position, it can feel like a betrayal of intimacy. Involving other people who were not present when the actual conflict occurred can create even further conflicts. This is especially true when those outside the conflict do not have all of the intimate and detailed history of the two people involved in the conflict; only one side is presented, or all of the facts are not presented or known. When you are brought into these situations, remain neutral, or you may find yourself alienating one or both parties when your opinions or remarks do not align with their expectations.

A series of unresolved conflicts can gradually escalate with time and erode the trust that forms the basis for intimacy. To start the process of resolution, *Adults* assume personal responsibility by being accountable for their part in any conflicts. Accountability may include apologies or actions that help heal conflicts when they arise. With personal responsibility and accountability, trust can be reestablished and deeper intimacy is allowed to develop through conflicts.

Betrayal of Intimacy

There are several ways in which intimacy is betrayed in relationships and creates distrust for future interactions. These include:

- Sharing private or confidential information
- Receiving personal information or witnessing intimate behavior that is then disclosed or gossiped to other people
- Being abrupt or rude in an intimate conversation
- Joking, banter, or sarcasm that is alienating, demeaning, or contains hurtful truths

- A partial or complete rejection of intimate words of affection or intimate behaviors by one of the parties involved
- Censorship or disallowing the expression of another's thoughts, views, or ideas.
- A series of lies, white lies or partial truths
- Taking unfair advantage of other people, using them or manipulating them.
- A series of unresolved conflicts
- A series of infidelities in a romantic relationship

When betrayal of intimacy does occur, these conflicts are best resolved with an apology and forgiveness to prevent resentment going forward and the harboring of conflicting emotions. Any betrayal requires a period of time to reestablish trust. The time required for healing a betrayal is determined by the level of betrayal, the number of times the betrayal occurred, and length of time in the relationship. Because intimacy develops from honesty and vulnerability, the level of betrayal should always determine the level of remedy provided. For healing to occur, it is required that the betrayal cannot happen again so that trust can be completely reestablished going forward. Extreme betrayals or multiple offensive betrayals can go well beyond reasonable near term forgiveness, or require termination of the relationship altogether in extreme circumstances.

Romantic Intimacy

A romantic relationship, while it includes sexual intimacy, also adds deeper and subtler layers of both complexity and the possibility for true fulfillment in relationship. The four most important factors for a successful intimate romantic relationship are open/honest communication, emotional intimacy, trust, and sexual intimacy. Open and honest communication leads the relationship into deeper emotional intimacy. Deeper emotional intimacy evolves as trust increases over time. With the development of deeper trust and increasing emotional intimacy, the relationship creates the foundation for sexual intimacy to occur.

Emotional intimacy can include any or all of the following: companionship, affection, shared goals, collaboration, support, shared interests, shared values and beliefs, and open communication and conversation.

Sexual intimacy includes sex and sexual connection, physical signs of affection such as hugs and kisses, and sharing intimate space together. Figure 1 shows how the elements of communication, intimacy, trust, and sex are related and form a continual loop that feeds each element for the ongoing health of a romantic relationship.

Any breakdown of any element in the loop of communication-intimacy-trust-sex usually affects the other elements of the loop depending upon when this occurs and the duration of the relationship. The most intense feelings of connection and gratification come through sexual intimacy when the elements of open/honest communication, emotional intimacy, and trust are present. Casual sex without the elements that deepen the sexual experience will gradually feel devoid of deeper meaning. Having casual sex or "friends with benefits" without emotional intimacy eventually feels empty and devoid of true feelings and emotions that form the basis of lasting romantic relationships. Such a connection may also be a way of using one another for sexual gratification when there is no intimacy or intent to move toward a committed relationship.

If the focus of the relationship is too much about sex, or sexual activity is desired too early in a relationship, this may be an indication that sexual gratification is all that is desired from the relationship. Having sex too soon without first developing some

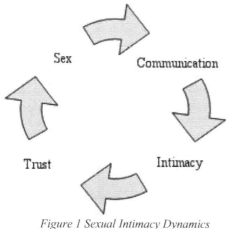

Figure 1 Sexual Intimacy Dynamics

87

degree of intimacy and trust can end the relationship early on. Developing the elements of true intimacy and trust first can lead to more meaningful sexually intimate experiences and provide the potential for a long-term relationship.

There is a balance between fulfilling your sexual desires and taking the time to develop deeper emotional intimacy and trust. If the decision to have sex is delayed by one partner in a romantic relationship, and there is a retreat or suspension of interactions from the other partner, this often indicates that sex was the only intention of the partner pulling away. Both partners must be comfortable, willing, and ready for sexual intimacy without feeling pressure or ulterior motives for sex beyond true affection and a desire for deeper intimacy. A romantic relationship containing all of the elements of mutual attraction combined with true affection will wait for sex until it feels right and feels comfortable for both people involved. While sex enhances a healthy relationship, it cannot be a replacement for the true intimacy that builds the foundation of a lasting relationship.

In romantic relationships, issues can arise requiring intimate conversations for resolution. If there is no private time for intimacy, then the relationship suffers. If a couple lives with other people or spends a great deal of time with other people, there may be little private time for intimate conversation and behavior. Lack of intimate time gradually takes its toll on the relationship. Time together alone as a couple in shared experiences together can rebuild the romantic intimate connection.

The decision to have premarital sex is based on each person's feelings and mutual agreements about how premarital sex is to be handled. Some couples choose to wait for marriage to have sex due to personal, religious, or societal beliefs. This can work if all of the other elements of communication, trust, and intimacy are present, and a strong sexual attraction is mutually felt before marriage.

Sexual compatibility is an important aspect in the early years of a healthy relationship, and there should be some consideration to having sex before marriage so each person can decide if they are sexually compatible as a couple. Everything from kissing to how much time is spent in foreplay and intercourse determines our sexual compatibility. Our desires for how a person feels, tastes, and smells are also components of our sexual compatibility, as well as how we "fit" together. Sexual compatibility is best explored when there are sincere desires for a lasting relationship and both feel sharing a sexual experience is appropriate to see if connection extends beyond mutual attraction to the physical level. Sex feels pleasurable in both the giving and receiving, so finding a partner who both gives and receives during sex makes these experiences enjoyable for both. When true affection exists, finding your partner's pleasure can also be great pleasure for you to give. This can take multiple sexual experiences to figure out what you like and what you don't like, as sexual expression can be extremely varied. Ultimately, love and deep intimacy unite to create a sacred sexual experience that is mutually fulfilling for both.

Either partner can initiate sex and either has the right to their individual response. However, continual denial of requests for sex without a legitimate reason will become negative reinforcement and cause potential problems for the relationship beyond sex. Some of the problems that can arise with repeated denial of sexual advances include feelings of resentment, not feeling attractive enough, suspicion of outside relationships, and lack of trust. Being open to having sexual intimacy, even if the result is simple acts of affection, keeps two people intimately connected in their relationship.

Sexual Intimacy

Intimate sexual relationships develop between consenting adults from an intimate connection that evolves over time. As previously mentioned, open and honest communication leads to emotional intimacy, and emotional intimacy leads to physical intimacy and sex. Any disconnect in the chain of honest and intimate communication can cause a breakdown of trust and problems in connecting sexually.

An open and intimate sexual relationship holds no limits to sexual expression: if it feels good, excites you and your partner, and is mutually respectful to both of you, then enjoy it! Negotiating what feels right and works best in a sexual relationship adds to the pleasure and diversity of sexual experiences over time.

Having sex without feelings of intimacy and affection is merely a sexual act for physical pleasure, which negates the emotional aspects leading up to a meaningful sexual experience. Sexual intimacy brings with it all of the emotional bonds that make the sexual experience fulfilling for both participants. The most demeaning relationship can occur when one partner is seen merely as a sexual object, and no true foundation of intimacy exists outside of sex. This sexual objectification is destructive to any relationship, and usually indicates that sex is the only objective in the relationship.

For a relationship to have any lasting meaning, it must combine the elements of romantic intimacy beyond the needs of sexual gratification. While prostitution is often considered sex for money, a truer meaning of prostitution may be the act of having sex with a person with no feelings of affection or intimacy. When you have a sexual relationship without intimacy, and the primary reason for sex is sexual gratification alone, financial support, money, or other provisions, this is prostitution. Prostitution becomes the ultimate subjugation of another human for pure physical pleasure, and for this reason is devoid of any real meaning or connection.

Sexual intimacy is not just the act of copulation or final orgasm. Sex can be any sensual act engaged either by yourself or with another consenting adult that satisfies your need for emotional intimacy, physical intimacy, or sexual desire. Sex can be spontaneous, planned, sensual, crazy, romantic, passionate, short, or long. It depends on the moment, the situation, and the needs of both consenting adults. You have to be slightly selfish to ask for what you want and desire during sex, but at the same time, give enough to provide for your lover's likes and desires. The best sex occurs when what you enjoy fulfills the needs and desires of your sexual partner, and your partner's needs and desires fulfill yours. Some people work well with routine sexual encounters, but similar to the diversity of foods we enjoy, a variety of sexual expressions can satisfy our appetite for sex, while also bringing great spontaneity and pleasure to the relationship. The best sex is probably expressed when there is a mixture of both routine and variety.

A sexual experience doesn't always have to end in an orgasm to be fulfilling. What you do before and after sex is just as important as the sexual act itself. The intimate conversations and expressions of affection allow us to feel cherished and loved. While the physical act of copulation or sexual orgasm brings wonderful physical intimacy, sexual intimacy also includes the pleasures of touching, kissing, and holding of one another that eventually lead to sexual arousal, sexual intercourse, and orgasm.

Your orgasm is not always the responsibility of your sexual partner in each sexual encounter. If we take care of ourselves just as much as we take care of the sexual needs of our partner, we will come away mutually satisfied more often than not.

How you begin and leave a sexual interaction is as important as the sexual act itself, and may be more important in the true expression of love and affection. Sexual banter and/or foreplay are important elements leading up to a sexual experience, as setting the stage for a meaningful sexual experience can be as exciting and intriguing as sexual orgasm together. After the sexual release, there can also be time for affectionate embraces and tender conversations. *Sexual Luminosity* is the period after all sexual activity has occurred in which lovers can share in the afterglow of physical release, love, connection, and affection that arose throughout their lovemaking. If one partner leaves this period after sex too quickly without the other partner's consent, this can result in feelings of discomfort or mistrust in the true intention of the sexual encounter.

Work toward an enjoyable sexual experience together, even if sharing mutual masturbation serves the intimacy needs of both people. With age it can take longer to have an orgasm, and while an orgasm can be extremely satisfying, other sensual elements and body contact become just as rewarding and intimate, releasing the goal of a final orgasm to have a fulfilling sexual experience. Removing the need or expectation that there must be a mutual orgasm lessens any pressure to perform or achieve something during sex and keeps the relationship open to the natural process of the body's needs. This allows the space for an orgasm to happen when the body is ready for the release.

Intimate sexual interactions are best kept private between the people involved. As previously stated, it can make people feel uncomfortable when they have to unwillingly see or hear physical or sexual intimacy, or even hear about it after the fact. It can also be a betrayal of intimacy with the person involved when you "kiss and tell" by telling other people about your intimate sexual experience. It also begs the question why there needs to be public displays of affection, as often these may be searches for public affirmation when a relationship, or a person in the relationship, is not secure in their personal intimacy. If a public interaction is getting sexually heated, then find someplace private to pick up where you left off. Your sexual encounters are best kept private with no one else present to observe or to hear your encounter. Keeping your sexual encounters private and personal will contribute to the sexual intimacy of the relationship over time.

CHAPTER SIX

Care and Maintenance of Relationships

Relationships do not always have to be hard work, but a relationship does require consistent care and maintenance to succeed. Relationships are like accounts you make deposits in along the way so you can reap the rewards and returns when you need the interest on your deposits. Similarly, you cannot withdraw more from a relationship than you put in. A life without the appropriate investment in relationships ends emotionally bankrupt. If we don't value and nurture our relationships throughout our lives, we can end up alone, going from one life experience to another by ourselves.

There are relationships in which those involved understand your needs; you understand theirs, and the relationship goes forward easily with minimal effort. Other relationships require more work and care to keep them intact, but you still find them worth the effort based on how they enrich your life. Many relationships may get off to a good start but then stall: they reach a non-working stage because neither person is willing to put forth the effort to maintain the relationship, or invest the energy it takes to end the relationship successfully.

A healthy relationship requires consistent care and maintenance, but the energy it takes for a relationship to fail is not always so obvious. A failed relationship requires emotional energy to process hurt feelings, grief, and loss, and the eventual letting go that must occur when it ends. Other areas requiring energy when romantic or more intimate relationships end are associated financial concerns and new living arrangements, all of which take time and energy to resolve.

As you engage in healthier relationships, you no longer step into the unhealthy roles of Victim, Persecutor, or Rescuer, thus avoiding unnecessary drama in your relationships. These three roles, common to many relationships, are known as "The Drama Triangle," first identified by transpersonal psychologist Stephen B. Karpman, M.D., and explored in more depth in Chapter Nine.[4] Beyond drama, we will also look at dysfunctional behaviors within relationships that do not nurture and sustain them, and the self-affirming behaviors that do sustain us in relationships.

Skillful conflict resolution is another element of healthy relationships and how each person approaches and resolves conflicts is the glue that keeps relationships healthy. Our ability to identify and resolve conflicts may be the most important skill we can learn for healthy long-term relationships.

In Chapter Five, we looked at how dealing with conflict can affect the level of intimacy in our relationships. Chapter Eleven explores in greater depth how to negotiate and navigate conflict resolution in relationships.

Eventually, every relationship has some disagreement to navigate, especially as closeness and duration increase. Those in healthy relationships understand that conflicts, even small ones, will naturally arise. If both people are willing to resolve the conflicts, no matter how large, the relationship can continue to experience deeper levels of intimacy and trust through the elements of kindness, consideration, honesty, and good faith, even in the midst of conflict.

Taking a good relationship for granted is one of the most common mistakes made in failing to care for and nurture a relationship. There is a mutual respect that develops in healthy relationships over time, for each other and for all the resources shared in the relationship. Gratitude maintains our connections through appreciation for what we give, and for what we receive. When we are grateful for another's time and resources and don't take them for granted, and they are grateful in return for our time and resources, the

---

[4] www.karpmandramatriangle.com

relationship experiences a continuum of mutual joy and gratitude for being in each other's lives. Sharing our resources becomes a natural give and take process that mutually sustains us.

The maintenance of healthy relationships requires not only that we joyfully celebrate the good times, but also that we show up with our willful support in the bad times. Relationships are about sharing the bad times and the good times, for better or for worse. Showing up for only one or the other does not serve the needs of a long-term relationship. Our life experience is the full range of both of these, and to deny any of these experiences is to deny the truth of what is the real human experience. Your best relationships share in the full spectrum of your life experiences.

Change is inevitable. Allowing two people in a relationship and the relationship itself to unfold, change, and grow may be one of the most important aspects of keeping a relationship new, interesting, and viable. Sometimes we grow apart or at different rates, and what seemed like it would last forever loses its luster when two people are not growing together or sharing in their growth together. Knowing how to negotiate change is an important aspect of caring for your relationships, as well as knowing each other's needs and negotiating fairly what can and cannot be given. Fair negotiation builds more trust over time, as disagreements inevitably arise, and the goal is to return to a position from which both parties win, or one or both parties are willing to compromise.

Relationships are built on the fulfillment of commitments. Fulfilling commitments is the regular care and maintenance that builds trust. We continually engage in agreements or commitments to one another, and fulfilling these commitments builds a lasting foundation of trust that continues to build over time. When commitments are failed, ignored, or disregarded in relationships, the relationship will feel disrespected, dishonored, and ultimately not trusted.

You cannot meet all of the expectations of even one person in your life, and one person cannot meet all of yours. Understanding this premise allows for fair and reasonable negotiations of expectations. Healthy relationships usually develop clear boundaries to indicate what is acceptable for the relationship and what is unacceptable, based on the length of the relationship. The setting, care, and maintenance of clear boundaries helps all involved in the relationship to know how to navigate fair and reasonable expectations.

To summarize, dysfunctional behaviors occur in relationships when interaction is based in drama; healthy boundaries are not respected; there is failure to keep commitments or a failure to honor the *Ten Elements of Healthy Relationships* (Chapter Three). We develop and maintain healthy relationships by engaging the following list of self-affirming behaviors:

- Learning to love yourself in relationship to others
- Allowing our relationships to grow and change over time
- Staying out of the drama roles (Rescuer, Victim, Persecutor) and moving to the healthier roles (Empathetic, Vulnerable, Decisive) when appropriate
- Setting clear boundaries for your needs
- Respecting the boundaries of others
- Making clear commitments
- Keeping your commitments
- Resolving conflicts fairly as they arise
- Managing fair and reasonable expectations
- Engaging in *The Ten Elements of Healthy Relationships*

Direct and Indirect Relationships

Your only business is your own direct connection with others, not the problems of their other (indirect) relationships. Staying out of the problems of other relationships is another critical factor in the care and maintenance of one's own relationships. Getting involved in the difficulties that arise from other people's relationships keeps your life complicated, emotionally difficult, and is a drain on your own primary relationships.

The only time being involved in someone else's relationship makes sense is when both parties in a given relationship have asked for your involvement, help, and/or support. We never fully know the past history of other relationships and therefore shouldn't make assumptions or judgments about anyone's current relationship behavior. All too often friends, spouses, or significant others feel compelled to give their opinions about others' relationships, knowing only one side of the story or knowing only some of the facts. Not only can this be inappropriate, but also it can lead to petty gossip rather than constructive help. Unsolicited feedback or unwanted help in solving these dilemmas often causes more problems than it solves. These are better left solved by the people in the direct relationship without outside involvement.

People often state they would like feedback on their personal relationships, but more often they just want to vent their frustration with a person or a particular situation or behavior. Learning to listen in these situations, not reacting too quickly, and not providing unwanted input serves your mutual advantage, especially when it becomes clear that others are just venting or stating facts. You can damage your relationships with others indirectly if you make negative or judgmental statements. An example: the individual who vented, may choose to continue with the relationship and perhaps relay your negative statements or judgments to the third person involved.

The exception to avoiding involvement in another's relationship is when you are asked for help in cases of emotional or physical abuse. If you are asked for input or help when the situation involves abuse or mistreatment, you have an obligation as an empathetic human being to provide assistance and support to the best of your ability, seeking professional help and assistance if required. In most circumstances of this nature, involvement is required.

When a couple engages with a friend who is a single person, some unique challenges may arise and need attention to ensure healthy and

97

enduring relationships, for the couple and for the friend. It often happens that a single person is already a friend of one person in the couple; however, being friends with both people requires some additional guidelines.

First, a couple must be secure in their own relationship, so neither is threatened by the single person's friendship. Each person is still responsible for their own one-to-one relationship, and each person has their own unique voice and presence amongst the three people involved. As well, if the single person feels obligated to interact with both people equally, show up for both equally, or provide gifts to both people in the couple, this results in a double burden. If couples expect a single person to contribute double their time, double their resources, and double their gifts, then a couple should double their efforts for gifts and resources provided.

Another aspect of supporting our relationships is to have someone we trust act as a "fair witness." A fair witness is a friend, a family member, or a trusted advisor who takes a position of telling us the truth. A fair witness helps us navigate life's conflicts and situations by providing the most truthful advice that can be provided, without taking sides and without judgment for what is presented. Trust is established through this provision of impartial truth, and mutual agreement to confidentiality. The fair witness does not just provide the advice you want to hear, but instead gives the advice containing the most truth. Becoming a fair witness is about helping others to see the truth in any given situation: not your beliefs nor your preferences, but the truth.

We are lucky if we have one or two fair witnesses in a lifetime. Most people will tell you what you want to hear, rather than what is hard, truthful, or may help you grow. Outside of close friends or family, a trained professional or a therapist can be a fair witness, if the individual is willing to engage actively in a process of exploring the truth of the situation.

Projection

One behavior that limits our possibilities for having healthy and intimate relationships with others is *projection*. Projection is the act of projecting beliefs onto another person, such as what they might be thinking or feeling, why they are behaving the way they are, or how they should respond in any given situation. Having an open and direct relationship without projection provides the foundation upon which healthy relationships can grow. Without projection, we engage directly in the moment and respond to what is occurring, not what we believe, or project, is occurring.

The truth is: engaging in projection during any interaction is only relating with ourselves in that moment. Rather than having a direct experience of the other person's thoughts and feelings in the present moment, we tend to project or overlay our thoughts, feelings, and beliefs, colored by our past experiences. Engaging in projection takes us out of direct relationship with another and instead engages us in a one-sided mental relationship with our beliefs and ideas about them. We may even take it as far as making decisions for them and deciding what we perceive they want for themselves; however, all of this is projection rather than sharing in the infinitely rich experience of engaging directly with a person's true nature and coming to understand their desires in the present moment.

Projection also can be an unconscious attempt to control another. In most interactions, there no is real intent to control, but rather a lack of awareness we are projecting our ideas onto another person or into a given situation. Projecting onto another person rather than engaging directly and openly further inhibits an authentic experience of relationship.

Projection may also arise from what is perceived as lacking, in need of attention, or problematic in the life of the person who is projecting. The person projecting will project their issues, either consciously or unconsciously, on to another person, where in reality, they are projecting what they need to look at within themselves.

Relationship occurs in the present moment when you have a direct experience of another person without projection. It unfolds spontaneously and changes or shifts as needed with the natural moment-to-moment flow of emotions, words, perceptions, behaviors and responses. Engaging directly also has the added benefit of freeing the other person and yourself from past behaviors or expected future behaviors based on past beliefs. This direct engagement in the present moment allows each person freedom to be who they truly are, not who you think they should be, not who you think they were in the past, not even who you think they are now. Understanding the mechanisms of projection, and catching oneself in the midst of projection, is an important key to creating *Adult* interactions that are engaging and meaningful.

The Importance of Priorities

With whom or on what we place our time and attention reveals everything about our priorities. We show through our actions, behaviors, and investment of our time and energy which relationships are important to us in our lives. While work, money, children, hobbies, travel, pleasure, and personal interests can be on our list of priorities, if we are attuned to what brings the most meaning to our lives, we find *people* mean the most to us and should always be our highest priority.

For any healthy and enduring relationship, we must get our priorities straight. If you place a higher value on anything other than your most cherished relationships, then there needs to be a reassessment of what is important to you. Your own personal health, well-being, and personal needs must always be considered in combination with the needs and priorities of those you care most about. You can put another's needs and priorities above your own needs temporarily, but if there is not the same or similar level of reciprocation, commitment, and priority, this won't work for the health of a relationship over the long term.

Priorities may change over time, but most people consider their relationships with their parents, spouses, significant others, or children as their highest priorities. In the list of priorities, romantic partners or spouses are usually at the top, and of course the needs of young children also have high priority, as this focus and attention provides the safe environment they need to develop a sense of belonging. Our chosen family of friends may attain a higher priority depending on the level of healthy Adult relationships we reach with our family of birth. Later in life, caring for the needs of aging parents may also take precedence and higher priority. Our priorities for the people in our lives are reflected through our actions and words in each interaction, so awareness of how we treat each other and how we are treated give us insight into our priorities and how to adjust them accordingly.

Showing Up

Showing up in other people's lives is about maintaining the continuity of being there in the good times as well as the hard times, which is important in the development of long-term relationships. There are tangible and intangible ways we show up for others by graciously giving of our time, money, energy, presence, love, affection, care, or support.

True compassion is expressed through our actions of showing up for others. Everyone goes through happy times and difficult times at some point in their lives. Showing up for them in both the good times and the bad times can be one of your greatest gifts to those you value in your life. When something traumatic does happen to someone in our lives or a real need exists, we can show up in simple ways with encouragement and words of kindness, and in more tangible ways with our time, money or energy. When there are great events or great news to share, then showing up for these also shows our care and support.

Showing up for large events of passage such as graduations, weddings, births, funerals, birthdays, anniversaries, and new homes is another way of acknowledging we care. There are also many small ways we can show up such as phone calls, emails to say we care, small gifts, and invitations to shared experiences. A big act or a gift is not always needed, but taking the time to write a card, make a call, or send a message, wishing a happy birthday or a happy anniversary is always much appreciated.

If you are not sure what to do or what to give for someone's birthday or anniversary, then ask them. They can provide options you are able to manage financially within the time required to put a gift together. Our birthday is the one day of year where it is about us, and it always makes us feel cherished by those adults in our lives who remember our birthdays and acknowledge remembrance with some act of kindness. There are enough calendars, Internet programs, and social media providing us with reminders so the task of having to commit birthdays to memory is no longer necessary.

If we only show up for each other when it is convenient or fun, or for our personal interests alone, we send a message that only good times or our individual personal interests matter. The relationship eventually suffers if bad times or shared interests are continually ignored for fun times and personal interests only.

Showing up through electronic devices or technology has some value, but nothing is more valuable than your physical presence. Showing up in person is not just the physical act of being together, but also clearing your mind of your own personal concerns, needs, and desires long enough so you can truly hear and be present for another person. Showing up must also be reciprocal and not just to benefit one person in the relationship the majority of the time.

Even though showing up should be reciprocal, expecting people to be there for us in ways they don't understand or ways in which they are incapable is unjustifiable. The best you can hope for in this situation is they are aware of their limitations and then show up in the best way they can. Managing our own expectations of how people can or will be present for us keeps us from having unhealthy or unrealistic expectations. Showing up for what are perceived needs, or showing up in ways that are convenient or easy rather than what is actually needed, is showing up at the most conveniently minimal level. Show up for what is needed, and if that is not known, then give it the consideration to ask what is needed.

Showing up and keeping commitments are related, but different: we can make a commitment to show up, but showing up doesn't always require a prior commitment. If people only show up in your life when they need your time, love, money, or other resources, then these relationships require too much energy to sustain them and suffer over time. Showing up is a mutually reciprocal activity that nurtures and sustains both sides of the relationship, not just one.

We can also show up for others by expressing our gratitude. Our gratitude for the value they bring to us through their love, their willingness to be there through the changing seasons of life and through their own continuous presence should be recognized and appreciated on a regular basis. Simple words of "thank you" and "I appreciate you" comfort us and sustain our willingness to reengage.

We need communities now in which people show up for the greater good, not just for their own good. Our relationships with friends and family suffer when we become too busy with jobs and immediate co-workers, and we don't attend to the regular tasks of showing we care and value our primary relationships. Being 'too busy' is rarely a valid excuse to fail in our relationships. There are a thousand ways, small and large, in which we can show up if we become observant. Showing up means making some effort, any effort and taking the appropriate action on a regular basis to show we care.

Life is a rich experience full of abundance, happiness, joy, sadness, and pain. Showing up at all of these experiences for others sustains and nurtures our connections. Show up and accept your part of this human condition, and trust the divine is always working perfectly. Enjoy your life and the people in it. Each day and each moment is a gift, as is each person in our lives. Taking our life, or the people in it, for granted may be the only true transgression. Show up and life will show you all it has to offer.

Gifts

Gift giving is another aspect of caring for and maintaining healthy relationships. The best gifts cannot be bought with money as they come from the heart. A true gift is given from the heart with no expectation of anything in return. Performing any act of kindness or gift giving with an expectation for the recognition it brings to the giver is giving under false pretenses. If you do have any expectation for a return on your gift, then this expectation is a form of co-dependent behavior.

Additionally, if any attached expectation accompanies a gift, the recipient will sense some form of indebtedness. A gift given with an expectation is not a gift, but rather a conditional agreement or contract for some future action or service. Both parties must agree to these types of expectations, or problems and discontent will develop when expectations are not fulfilled. While conditional giving is applicable to contracts, such as your job or employment agreement, conditional giving is not always appropriate in personal relationships, as these are based more on reciprocity in relationships over time. Gifts that serve to accommodate the needs and desires of others are perfect when you feel this is best for you, for the other, and for the relationship. Giving out of a sense of obligation, however, lessens the joy of giving and receiving. Make sure the person who wants affection or other favors in return for their gifts understands that beyond your gratitude and thankfulness, you cannot be obligated to them.

Gifts become a representation of love when we are young, but as we mature, gifts representing our love are much different. No external gift can replace loving acts by another, or the gift of another's presence when needed.

The gift of shared experiences together make lasting memories. No gift can surpass the gift of showing up and being completely present for those we care for and love. While our world thrives on external material gifts, these can never bring us the lasting happiness we seek.

Gift giving that is limited to gifts from sustainable resources includes the additional gift to the earth of not over-consuming her resources. When giving gifts, a consideration for what is needed most versus the capitalist criteria for what cost the most or is purely luxury moves us out of wasteful spending and wasteful gift giving.

The best gifts are those that result from intentional thought and consideration. A gift that shows an investment of thoughtful effort, planning, and time can be more loving and caring than a gift purchased gratuitously. What you give may not be as important as how it is given, including the thoughtfulness, time, and love utilized in preparation of the gift. Some of the gifts money cannot buy include our time, our care, our support, our advice, and our willingness to be there in times of need. Our greatest gift may always be the simple act of showing up and being there for those we love with our time, attention, and care. One of the greatest gifts can be when someone recognizes a need and steps in to take care of it without being asked and without any expectation of anything in return. The next best gift is when you do ask someone to help, and they accept gladly and provide the help needed.

Misunderstandings arise when there is no clear concept of what is given as a gift and what is loaned. Loaned items are not gifts and become stolen items if the loaned item is not returned. A person who redefines a personal item loaned as a gift cannot be trusted with future loaned items again.

A gift is not a gift if it is not willingly received. If someone explicitly asks not to receive a gift for an occasion, then honor their request. An unsolicited or unwelcome gift can cause feelings of guilt or regret if the recipient is unable or unwilling to return the favor and give a gift in kind. A gift denied or not received can also reflect an unwillingness to engage in relationship. Our willingness to receive a gift shows our graciousness and willingness to engage in the relationship. When unsolicited gifts are received, don't let the feeling of embarrassment for the gifts overtake your ability to say thank you and express gratitude.

People can have issues about the giving and receiving of gifts. There are those who give gifts to receive affection or other favors in return. Low self-esteem or a low self-worth may prevent some people from receiving gifts. Be sensitive to either of these situations in gift giving, and help the person with low self-esteem feel valued and loved by your gift. If gifts are truly not wanted, or there is no willingness to receive the gifts offered, then this request is best honored and not pursued further.

We are all given personal gifts or talents unique to each one of us. What you do with your gifts or talents brings joy to you and to those who experience your gifts. A personal gift is only appreciated and received when its true value is realized, accepted, and nurtured. Not everyone will understand the gifts and talents you share with them, nor appreciate them. Give your gifts to those who will appreciate them, or like "pearls before swine"[5] your gifts will be unappreciated, and your efforts will be wasted.

Respect and be gracious for each and every gift that comes your way. Gifts return to us through the giving of the gift, the receiving of the gift, and the value or use of the gift once given. Save your gifts for those who willingly give and willingly receive, including those who will appreciate your gifts.

Gratitude

Living in a state of gratitude for all the gifts life presents to us is important, as this brings us into harmony with the natural flow of the universe. *Our gratitude for what is received opens up the potential for us to receive more.* When we are bitter, ungrateful, or passive about life's gifts, we

---

[5] The Holy Bible, King James Version, Matthew 7:6, *Sermon on the Mount*

remove ourselves from the natural flow of the divine fulfilling our desires in each moment we experience. Take time each day to experience gratitude for someone, something, or some aspect of your life. By living in conscious gratitude, you give energy to what you are thankful for and provide a rich environment for more of these gifts to manifest in your life. Expressing gratitude each day changes one's whole approach to living. Taking life for granted or the gifts we receive begrudgingly, attracts more limitation to our living.

In our relationships, we can show how we appreciate the love and generosity given to us by others by giving back to them in kind, or by showing our gratitude with each act of kindness. One of the many gifts of appreciation you can give another person is the knowledge that you need and value the relationship you have with them, including, what value this individual brings to your life.

When you ask for or are given another person's time, knowledge, professional advice, or other resources, offer some accommodation for that person's generosity, even if only through your gratitude. Your appreciation for the resources can be in the form of a small gift, a dinner, your time to help them, or money for business relationships. Your graciousness is appreciated and has the added value of continuing the flow and development of the relationship. When you forget or do not thank someone for gifts, the omission sends a message that the gifts are not appreciated or valued, as most of us have experienced at some point when not thanked for the gifts we have given.

Mistakes are made when people with position or affluence are perceived to not need gifts of gratitude. We all appreciate being thanked for the resources we provide to others and to not be thanked leaves one feeling unappreciated and taken for granted.

The time to express your thanks is as soon as possible after receiving a gift. Don't let too much time go by without saying thank you for what was given. If you wait too long to show your thanks, your gratitude is diminished and looks more like an afterthought or even a form of disrespect for either the person or the gift given.

Be grateful for what you have right now and do not wait until it is removed to appreciate your gifts. Be thankful each day for all you have, if only for simply living another day. If you are reading these pages then you have been given the human powers of reasoning and self-awareness to seek knowledge in this lifetime for a greater understanding and awareness of life. Not every person or every being is given this gift, so be in gratitude for these gifts of reasoning and self-awareness. Our gratitude and thankfulness brings more to us of what we are thankful for. While hindsight can teach us thankfulness for what we had, we forget to express gratitude for what is occurring now. Gratitude for present moments sows fertile ground for our future desires. Be in gratitude for your life, including all the good, all the bad, and all the ugly. This energy of gratitude for what you have brings more of what you have, so practice gratitude regularly and often. We often don't know what we have until it is gone. Be grateful today for the gift of your life, including your relationships and all the abundance of life given to you.

Never take long-term relationships for granted and forget how to appreciate the people who show up for you each day. Too often we become passive and take the people who have been beside us for all those years for granted, not remembering what a gift they are to our lives.

The universe always gives to us, but sometimes our interpretation of its gifts may be a perception of something being taken away from us, such as when the death of a loved one is perceived as tragic. But often here too, many gifts of love come from those who are witnessing the dying process, as well as the gifts experienced by the one who is transitioning. Death is one more example of how life gives to us all of the time when we are willing to see its gifts.

Be grateful for *all* the gifts we receive, both large and small, in whatever circumstances or packages they come. Life provides us with gifts in each day and in each moment if we are present enough to see them. Often what we perceive as a negative circumstance is actually a gift, if only we can recognize it. Sometimes we won't recognize the gifts we received until we are able to look back at these in hindsight.

Graciousness

Graciousness is the art of making other people feel comfortable and appreciated. Graciousness encompasses several behaviors, including respect, consideration, gratitude, empathy, and compassion for others. It also includes such skills as dealing tactfully with people, respecting others' boundaries, being welcoming and hospitable, and showing concern and care for others and their needs.

Graciousness is about learning to value the needs of others and balancing their needs with yours. This means sometimes we get the best seat in the house, and other times we are willing to let another have the place of honor. When a person experiences difficult life challenges, the kindest minimal extension of care is to tell them they are in your thoughts and you wish the best for them. Not knowing what to do is never a valid excuse for doing nothing.

Graciousness is also about giving credit where credit is due and is one more way to show support of others. Everyone responds positively to sincere praise and appreciation. Taking credit for another's work, ideas, or actions is undermining and disregards the value that was provided. Sharing credit or giving credit when and where it is due is always appropriate and gracious.

Graciousness also means you are able to give your gifts or resources to another person without resentment or complaints. Before you give a gift or resource to another, be sure you can give it freely and graciously without any feelings of resentment after the gift is given. If you cannot give a gift in a gracious manner, then consider not giving gifts in the future. A gift that is given ungraciously is not a gift at all.

When you visit someone in their home, their city, or their country, always be respectful of their space and country of residence. Words, actions, or behaviors that disrespect or devalue their home, space or country in any way are best avoided. We build bridges and remove boundaries when we are open and willing to understand and embrace the differences of other peoples and other cultures.

When you invite someone into your home or personal space, be gracious, warm, welcoming, and accommodating while that person shares your space. When someone invites you as a guest in their home or personal space, then be respectful and caring of their space and time, carefully leaving it in the same or better order than you found it. A gracious guest knows how to show up on time and also how to leave on time and not overstay their welcome. Graciousness is about becoming more sensitive to another person's needs and accommodating those needs as one can. A guest's visit of three days and three nights staying in someone's home is plenty. Beyond this, the stay can become difficult for the routines of the household and cause people to over-extend their generosity beyond what is comfortable. A gracious host makes a gracious guest. Be a gracious host, but also a gracious guest and do not overstay your welcome.

Another way in which we can be gracious is by showing respect for people's privacy, their private business and personal information. Asking too many questions, making invasive statements or exposing private matters alone or in public is distasteful and can lead to feelings of mistrust and betrayal.

Being gracious requires equality and humility. Humility is the antidote to the ego's need to separate itself by being better than others. Equality is the antidote to the ego's need to separate by feeling entitled. Both humility and equality open our hearts to understand we are all connected as one people, as well as demonstrate that we value equity and justice for all. We become *humanists*, rather than *individualists* seeing only the interest of any special group that segments or creates division of people. As you become an *Adult*,

110

your equality and humility grow into more graciousness. The ego no longer demands that its needs be met over the needs of others, nor does it subjugate itself to another's egoic demands.

CHAPTER SEVEN

Commitments

A *commitment* is an agreement you make with yourself or another being, for a specific resource, action, or behavior to occur at a specific time, for a period of time, or forever from a point forward. Keeping your commitments is one of the primary foundational behaviors of an *Adult* and builds respect and trust in relationships. Relationships gain forward momentum from agreements and commitments that are honored and realized.

The first step we look at is how to make commitments that are fair to others and fair to ourselves. The next step is learning how to act responsibly to fulfill the commitments we make. Finally, we look at how to manage and keep our commitments, and when it is appropriate to break a commitment.

Before any commitment is kept or fulfilled, there must first be a desire by one or both parties to make a commitment. The forming of a commitment can move logically from an idea, to tentative plans, to firm plans, to an invitation, and finally to a commitment. Whenever you become clear you are willing and able, skip the interim steps and move directly to making the requested commitment. Commitments are made voluntarily between the people involved without using manipulation or guilt as a means to have a commitment fulfilled.

Commitments should always be clear statements of intention. A clear commitment always states how, when, or where the resource or behavior will occur without ambiguity. It is not possible to make a commitment if the date, time, specifics of the commitment, or desired outcomes are not known. Ambiguous commitments cause more confusion and turmoil requiring extra time and energy to clarify what is needed to proceed. Ambiguity can be a way of avoiding commitment or an attempt to gain more leverage from a commitment when it is finally made.

Making tentative plans means one or both parties are not yet willing to make a commitment. Tentative plans take extra time and energy while everyone goes into a holding pattern to figure out if they will keep the commitment or not. All parties involved must agree to the making of tentative plans because doing so usually involves holding a time available in the future and requires more negotiation for the event to occur. Tentative plans can work if they are for a brief period while everyone checks their schedules to insure they are free. Tentative plans that are tentative up to the time of the event indicate an unwillingness to commit.

The types of commitments are time commitments, behavioral commitments, and binding commitments. We commit our time and resources to many people in our lives including our friends, our family, our jobs, and even ourselves. There are certain behavioral commitments we make, such as showing up on time for work or being monogamous in a sexual relationship. We also engage in binding commitments such as agreeing to a mortgage loan, paying off credit cards, marriage, confidentiality, work contracts, or other commitments requiring civil or legal agreements. Whatever the type of commitment being considered, enter it consciously with a true desire to fulfill the obligation to yourself and to the people involved, or decide not to make the commitment at all. *Adults* honor and keep the commitments they make.

Anytime an agreement is broken there is usually some form of confusion, upset or conflict. When small commitments are not respected or fulfilled, these small failures can lead to doubt about a person's ability to keep larger or more important commitments. In a sense, repeated failures to keep commitments is a red flag indicating that the person is not an integrated *Adult* or does not value the relationship enough to keep their commitments. Words of commitment become irrelevant over time if there are no corresponding actions to support them.

Time is one of our most valuable resources, and respecting our time commitments to others and ourselves will always serve us well. One of the most common commitments we make on a daily basis is agreeing to be somewhere or meet someone at a particular time. If we could just show up to work or for other events whenever we felt like it or wanted, then commitments would not be needed. Living in this world as an *Adult* means we take responsibility for managing our time, respecting the time of others, and knowing where and when we are to show up. Showing up on time indicates respect for the relationship and the understanding that the other person's time is as valuable as our time. Taking time commitments seriously is the behavior of an *Adult*. Failing to take time commitments seriously erodes our ability to generously give our time or make time commitments. Becoming a responsible *Adult* means you show up on time for the commitments you make.

The first step in learning to make and keep commitments is keeping the personal commitments we make with ourselves. This is imperative for the development of the love and respect you have for yourself. Keeping self-commitments also teaches us how to make, keep, and respect our commitments to others.

How Commitments Affect Our Relationships

An *Adult* sets clear commitments with others to maintain healthy relationships. This means setting clear agreements for how, when, or where commitments will be fulfilled. Making clear commitments eliminates misunderstandings, ambiguity, and hurt feelings. Additionally, asking for an agreement will likely be more successful than making demands.

By keeping commitments in relationships *Adults* show themselves and other people the respect, integrity, and love they have for themselves, for each other, and for their relationships. *Commitments are concentric to integrity.* You honor other people when you keep your commitments to them, just like you honor yourself when you keep commitments to yourself.

The time between making a commitment and the time when the actual commitment takes place is rich with possibilities. Once we make a commitment, we have a period of looking forward to the event, then sharing the experience of the event when it actually arrives, and finally enjoying the memory of the event and the commitment we shared subsequent to the event. Keeping commitments should not bind us, ingratiate us or obligate us begrudgingly. We should enter into any commitment we make willingly or not at all. Avoiding making commitments or breaking commitments detracts from our relationships and does not establish the rich ground needed for potential experiences we can share through the commitments we make with others.

Making and keeping commitments with one another is a co-creative process, and when we fulfill those commitments, we create a sense of assurance. On the other hand, when commitments are not made and getting together is random, or commitments are made and then broken, we experience feelings of betrayal and distrust in addition to feeling guarded with the person going forward. Many may think making and keeping commitments will limit their lives in some way, but in reality commitments are sacred acts that bring us together, sustain our connections, and fulfill our desires.

For all of these reasons, making and keeping commitments cultivates trust and enhances respect in our relationships. There will always be circumstances that make it impossible to keep our commitments to others. When this happens it is most effective to notify people truthfully and as soon as possible, why you cannot keep the commitment, and present terms of a new commitment when appropriate.

Promises are commitments, agreements, or pledges that a particular behavior or event will occur, or a past behavior or event will no longer occur. Promises made without the corresponding actions taken to fulfill those promises are empty promises. Unfulfilled promises are a type of failed commitment carrying the same consequences as broken commitments. It is better to not make a promise, rather than overpromise, make a promise that you cannot fulfill or do not intend to fulfill.

Reciprocal commitments are commitments we make with others with a shared sense of responsibility. A reciprocal commitment is often conditional, such as "I will do this for you, if you will do this for me." Reciprocal commitments work well if both parties agree to the reciprocal terms of the commitment, and the terms are equitable for those involved. A question you can always ask when a commitment with another arises is this: "Would this person make this same commitment to me in return?" If your answer is ambiguous, then make the commitment and see if there is reciprocity in the relationship over time. If the answer is "No," there is no need to feel obligated to make the corresponding commitment.

There are people who choose not to make commitments; they prefer to live life spontaneously. There is nothing wrong with living in the moment or being noncommittal, if it doesn't involve other people. However, relationships usually work better when there is a clear intent by all involved to make and keep the commitments made. Try showing up whenever you want for work, and you will find yourself unemployed. Similarly, we don't just get to go in and out of people's lives in a spontaneous way as it suits us. There can be a fine line between living spontaneously and an unwillingness to become an *Adult* who is able and willing to make and keep commitments.

Just because others fail to keep their commitments to you does not mean you are to respond by failing to keep your commitments to them as punishment. It is better not to make a commitment than to fail to keep a commitment once made.

In addition to our human relationships, we may have commitments to other living beings on this planet such as the animals, the forests, and the planet itself. Every living being has its place and value in this world, and we are all connected. If commitments are made to take animals as pets, then honor those commitments to care for, nurture, and provide for them until their death. Making and keeping commitments to ourselves, our relationships, our

116

work, and other beings bring peace and harmony to our lives and the world around us.

Invitations

An invitation is the precursor for a commitment. How we handle the acceptance of an invitation, or how we extend invitations enhances our relationships with trust and respect. Invitations can also reveal where you stand in relationship to the priorities of other people. When we show up for others at the request of their invitations, we may experience a natural desire for reciprocity. Reciprocity in invitations makes both people feel valued in the relationship. If, on the other hand, only one person is initiating invitations, this may be an indication that the relationship is either not a priority or not important enough for invitations to be extended.

Clear invitations tend to unite; ambiguous invitations tend to separate. Ambiguous invitations or invitations without clear directions or parameters for engagement are declined more often than those that are specific. Invitations that clearly state the date, the time, the duration, and any resources required for the event are more likely to be accepted. The further into the future an event is happening, the greater the possibility that people will be able to accept the invitation. Sending invitations as soon as possible and following up with reminders closer to the event help keep everyone informed and gives people plenty of time to respond, make plans, or rearrange plans to attend.

If an invitation includes financial obligations, any money required or associated charges should be clearly stated. Committing people to financial obligations they may not have the means to meet is unfair. Anyone being extended an invitation has the right to know if they are required to provide any resource in addition to their time and presence at an event.

The people who are invited to an event is the business of the host(s). It is impolite and inappropriate to invite people to an event that you are not hosting without first obtaining approval from the host. Doing so can lead to

117

uncomfortable situations with you and the host. There may be limitations on food or seating, or the host may simply not want to invite other people. Consideration should be given to inviting both members of a couple when social invitations are extended, rather than only one of the pair. In this way, both people feel included in events that involve other couples.

Responding to an invitation in the moment with a clear "yes" or "no" gives everyone involved the information they need to know for the event. A "yes" or "no" can pertain to all or part of an invitation. Responding "yes" to the entire invitation and then wanting to remove parts of it later can be awkward and change the terms of the initial invitation. Be clear and up front regarding what you are agreeing to or accepting in an invitation, whenever possible.

Response time to invitations is important: how quickly we respond shows we care and are interested in attending the event. Long lapses in time to respond may indicate disinterest or indifference. Plans can also change considerably or become irrelevant if there is too much wait time for a response. However, being flexible regarding changes in invitations to events that are large or involve a lot of people shows your interest and support for the person extending the invitation.

Even if you have to decline an invitation, responding graciously to let the person who invited you know you cannot attend shows that you honor and respect that person and your relationship. If you would like to be invited again, mention this and ask to consider another time or ask for a rain check. This shows interest to engage again while complete disregard of an invitation shows lack of interest and disrespect.

Too often today, a lack of any response is considered an appropriate response to an invitation. It is not. If a person took the time to invite you, then a reply of simply "No, I won't be able to attend" is the most respectful response to their generosity and consideration. If they cared enough to invite you, it is important to care enough to respond in kind. If you are not able to accept an invitation, and then on top of that you also don't respond, it can feel like a double insult. A response shows respect for the individual extending the invitation, and at a minimum, an acknowledgement of that person's intrinsic value as a human being.

If the original invitation plans become ambiguous, shift, or change over time, you have the right to change an initial response of "yes" to a "no," or to request more information. Making changes to plans or assumptions that involve another person's schedule without first confirming their availability may result in disappointment or hurt feelings. If your response to an invitation is dependent on other conditions, be clear about those conditions so that people can respond or plan accordingly.

It is also not appropriate to ask who is attending an event or to make your presence dependent upon who else is attending. If you are invited to an event, and friends or others with whom you would not be comfortable will be present, then thoughtfully decline the invitation for personal reasons. If you care for the host, but know that such a situation is probable, then either put your feelings aside and attend the event to be respectful to the host, or decline the invitation and explain why attending would have been difficult for you.

Invitations that are conditional or used to shame or guilt a person into coming, such as, "I will be hurt if you don't show up," or "Please don't disappointment me," put unnecessary conditions on the invitation. Similarly, imposing conditions before accepting an invitation such as, "Could I bring my friend?" are unfair and improper.

Additionally, it is inappropriate to believe that everyone should or could be invited to all events all of the time. While intentionally excluding someone from an invitation who would normally be invited is unfair and may be passive aggressive, there is no appropriate response other than personal disapproval. Everyone cannot be invited to every event, and an *Adult* understands that not being included in a group invitation is usually not meant to be a personal slight. Feeling hurt when we do not receive an invitation becomes a waste of emotional energy. How we handle extending invitations keeps the process of making commitments in our relationships healthy and dynamic, while how we receive and respond to invitations displays how we value and cherish our relationships.

When Commitments Fail

Keeping commitments to oneself and to others is a fundamental element of living as a responsible *Adult*. Responsible *Adults* sign up for those responsibilities they know they can keep, they plan to fulfill, and they will follow through on. When they cannot fulfill a commitment, there is a corresponding apology, actions to right any resultant negative consequences, and an action to recommit. Living as a responsible *Adult* alleviates unnecessary stress and drama in your life because it is always clear that you show up for commitments you make, or you do not make commitments you cannot keep.

If you have failed to keep a commitment, apologize immediately, and then make amends. One of the ways we can make amends is to make a clear statement of recommitment immediately. If someone else is the offender, look to see how they handle the failed commitment, the nature of their explanation, and the immediacy of the response. An *Adult* responds to any failed commitment with a timely apology for not following through. A responsible *Adult* is honest, tells you exactly what happened, and any corresponding reasons why they failed to keep their commitment. If the individual values and respects the relationship, the corresponding apology or amends to any failed commitment will be made as quickly as possible.

If a friendship or a romantic relationship is fairly new, breaking a commitment without a valid excuse is usually more serious. The failures to keep small commitments at the beginning of a relationship may indicate future problems to come.

If you break a commitment and do not notify the other person of the change in plans, the individual may feel undervalued or that their time is not important. Last minute cancellations can be the worst failure in breaking a commitment, as the other party has then lost the chance to schedule valuable time elsewhere. If we expect others to make and keep their commitments to us, then we must also walk our talk, and behave the way we would want and expect others to behave regarding commitments.

If you find you have inadvertently double booked yourself, it is more appropriate to keep the first commitment made. If this is not possible, then graciously admit to both parties you have mistakenly double booked and ask for their help and flexibility in finding a solution for which commitment to keep.

However we handle our commitments, whether with failure or with follow through, commitments provide the continuous feedback that allows us to get clear priorities and how to respond in the future. None of us is at the top of everyone's priority list, and to expect this is unreasonable. We can and should expect to be treated fairly and with respect in regards to invitations extended and any co-commitments made. The way we make and keep commitments to one another is a result of knowing our relationships and determining their priorities.

There is also the situation of a commitment being cancelled so that a better offer can be accepted. Canceling one offer in order to accept a better offer is always rude and offensive. Accepting a better offer is one of the most insulting ways to break a commitment. It shows that the person does not value the friendship or relationship enough to make a firm commitment and would rather wait to see if another invitation comes in they would enjoy more. The regular use of tentative plans instead of firm commitments can be a setup for this *"better offer"* syndrome. The *better offer* syndrome is best discussed directly if the better offer is suspected or revealed. Related to the "better offer" is the reluctance to commit for fear of missing out-*FOMO*-on something better, but what? What is more important than the person who has stepped up and wants to make a commitment to share time or an experience with you now? When a person sets up an ambiguous commitment such as "Let's wait and see if I am available at that time," be clear you consider the time uncommitted and will pencil them in or make other plans. At least with this approach there is fairness, and you are both free to accept a better offer if one arises. Any type of ambiguous commitment is really no commitment at all. If ambiguous commitments happen repeatedly, then at some point an honest conversation is needed to discuss that this sort of arrangement does not work. A direct discussion on whether or not the relationship is important enough for the person to make a clear commitment can clarify priorities and how to proceed going forward. This conversation has the added benefit of showing the person how their inability to commit does not honor or respect the relationship.

You may sometimes find yourself engaged with people who ask for large commitments from you and who in return offer small commitments by comparison, or they may regularly fail to keep even minor commitments. This failure of the balance of reciprocal level of commitments erodes trust in the relationship over time. Such an imbalance can be addressed by stepping back to equitable levels of commitments in the relationship until both are ready to make larger commitments.

We are human and fail our commitments to others at some point in our lives. Taking steps to acknowledge our failures, to explain, and to apologize helps to clear the air completely, shows respect for the person involved, acknowledges the value of the relationship and the other person's time, and avoids residual unresolved feelings. When you are willing to take personal responsibility for commitments you keep, and commitments you fail, you show those involved you are a responsible *Adult* worthy of merit in relationships.

CHAPTER EIGHT

Healthy Boundaries

Healthy boundaries make for healthy relationships, but what is a boundary, exactly, and how are boundaries beneficial?

Boundaries are guidelines or protocols of engagement for how we are to interact together in safe, reasonable, and respectful ways. Healthy boundaries tell other people how to interact with you with consideration for the needs of everyone involved. Healthy boundaries can be limits we set for ourselves (personal boundaries) or limits we set with others (interpersonal boundaries). Personal boundaries require that we become clear about who we are and what we want for ourselves in each moment. Interpersonal boundaries require that we become clear about what we want and expect from others. The clearer you become about your personal boundaries, the healthier your interpersonal boundaries with others become, because people will understand what to expect from you, how to interact with you, and how to honor and respect boundaries that are reasonable and fair.

Healthy personal boundaries are an expression of what you want for yourself or don't want for yourself. It is our personal responsibility to inform others of our boundaries and to enforce our boundaries with others. They let others know what you desire from them and from the relationship. It is when we cross boundaries or do not respect boundaries that cause conflicts to begin to arise. Healthy boundaries provide guidelines for how we can come together in healthy interactions; they are not rules for separation.

Boundaries cover a whole gamut of circumstances from large to small. Smaller boundaries may include something as simple as asking a friend not to engage you in idle gossip about a mutual friend. Larger boundaries may require suspending a relationship for a period of time to see if healthier behaviors can be reestablished in the relationship.

Getting clear on boundaries isn't always possible in the moment, but as we apply more effort toward understanding our personal needs and desires in our interactions, we become clear about what we want for ourselves and how to set boundaries which reflect those needs and desires. Practicing self-awareness around what we desire has the effect of bringing us closer to responding in the moment to boundary issues. Our best response to boundary issues takes place the moment they arise, rather than later or in hindsight when memories do not always serve both parties equally. You cannot change what happened in past interactions, but you can set healthy boundaries for how you are to interact going forward.

Our personal boundaries define how we move through the world and how we limit certain behaviors to protect us or keep us healthy and whole. Healthy personal boundaries can help us achieve our goals and successes. They can teach us how to avoid spreading our time or energy too thinly across too many interests, to the point where everything of value in our lives suffers. Focusing on the completion of tasks and limiting the amount of additional commitments we make to others and ourselves helps us set appropriate boundaries for our time and resolve multi-tasking nightmares.

By defining clear boundaries, we communicate our preferences for interacting in relationships. Boundaries can be set with kindness and consideration for everyone involved, without the need for off-putting words that are harsh or rude. For boundaries to be honored, however, they must first be reasonable, fair, and mutual for everyone involved. Our healthiest position in a relationship occurs when we honor and respect fair and reasonable boundaries. Setting clear boundaries at the beginning of relationships creates a foundation of mutually respected needs for the relationship. Clear boundaries up front give people clarity to see if, how, or when they want to engage. Too many boundaries too early will be too constrictive, and boundaries that are too strict or are unfair or unreasonable will cause others to retreat or be tentative in their engagement. Setting too many boundaries can also become exhausting and may indicate the relationship is not working

124

for either one or both people involved. On the other hand, too much flexibility or over-allowance can enable behaviors you eventually regret and require boundaries be established or reset.

As our relationships deepen over time, and we gain greater understanding of another's behaviors, our needs—regarding how we want to engage with that person going forward—may change or become clearer. Boundaries may be renegotiated and reestablished to reflect those changing needs. Each person is responsible for openly discussing their needs and boundaries as they arise. By considering and adjusting to everyone's needs for change, the relationship keeps moving forward.

Some relationships require minimal or no boundaries, because there is intuitive understanding of healthy boundaries as well as sensitivity to each other's needs. Most boundaries are implicitly understood by each other's words, actions, or behaviors. These can be our easiest relationships because boundaries are mutually understood from the beginning of the relationship. These "easy" relationships are rare, however, and at some point there is the need for new boundaries or a need for existing boundaries to be renegotiated. Many people need explicit boundaries set, with corresponding agreements mutually understood and respected, before they can move forward with the relationship. Unclear, ambiguous or misunderstood boundaries need a verbal explanation to keep everyone informed about what is needed without leaving them to guess what is needed, or assume what is required.

Boundaries can be specified for any of our personal resources: the giving of our time, money or energy, sharing of personal space, how we want to communicate, what behaviors we desire, and how we are to respect privacy are a few. Boundaries can be subtle, such as determining when to spend time together, or they can be more direct, such as limiting the use of abusive or offensive words in your presence. A boundary can also be a statement to someone about how their future actions or behaviors will affect you or make you feel, especially when these actions or behaviors are potentially hurtful or could have a negative impact on you.

When a boundary is set with intent and conviction, there is less ambiguity and a better chance others will understand what is needed and desired. You are entitled to set boundaries for your own personal desires, your views, and how you spend your time, money, and energy, as is everyone else around you. Certain boundaries require no room for negotiation, no change of position. Other boundaries are up for discussion and negotiation, recognizing that boundaries are guidelines, not rules.

It might seem that healthy boundaries would limit one's involvement in healthy relationships, but quite the opposite is true. Healthy *Adults* have healthy boundaries. Setting healthy boundaries has the effect of allowing one to engage with many different types of people, because when healthy boundaries are in place, people are clear about how to relate with you and how you are to relate with them. When people have boundaries that are unclear, ambiguous, or nonexistent, interacting with them can be more challenging or difficult. Without clear boundaries, these individuals don't know what they want for themselves, and you don't know the parameters for how to interact with them resulting in guesswork at what is actually expected of you. Clear boundaries are often all that is needed to clear up ambiguity in our relationships.

People who don't understand the need for personal boundaries or don't respect another's boundaries may feel hurt, disappointed, or distanced by boundaries. Too often we personalize boundaries to mean rejection, but this is not always the case. Fair and reasonable boundaries are mutually beneficial to those involved in healthy relationships. They are best accepted and agreed upon without being taken personally. Learning to set and accept the boundaries of others without personalizing them allows relationships to develop based on the transparency of each person's desires being known, understood, and respected.

Boundaries can be more difficult to set with a person when you fear you will let a person down or disappoint them. In reality and more importantly, you let yourself down when you give too much, allow more than you feel you

126

can or should, or are not authentic in expressing your needs or desires. Without healthy boundaries, we can find ourselves over-giving, over-extending or over-allowing, and with time this creates more problems and can eventually lead to feelings ranging from mild annoyance to resentment.

Most relationships will only require negotiation of boundaries at the onset of the relationship, but some relationships will require continual maintenance of boundaries. If boundaries are continually crossed or continuously failed, then this can indicate 1.) a person's lack of respect for boundaries, 2.) a lack of knowledge about the importance of boundaries, or 3.) an unwillingness to engage in healthy boundaries. These relationships can take too much time and energy to maintain. Either you change to minimize or disallow the boundaries you have set, or others change to agree to your boundaries. Those relationships unwilling or unable to engage in the process of negotiating fair and reasonable boundaries probably won't last.

Whenever you begin to engage with someone, your responsibility is to determine if boundaries are needed and then set clear boundaries up front. There are always early signals of any boundaries that will need to be set. Doing so gives everyone involved the choice to accept your boundaries or choose to do otherwise. A classic example is the prospect of a family member coming to stay for three weeks in your home. Your busy work schedule will not leave you with enough time and energy to be a gracious host and entertain. You can simply tell the person this will not work and offer a stay of five days if this is the best you can do. Another way to handle such a situation is to tell the family member this is a busy time in your life, and they are welcome to stay for this long, but you will continue with your work schedule, and will happily share dinners and evenings together. Boundaries with caveats can supply further definition and meaning, make the limits less formal, and/or lessen their severity.

Setting boundaries is not required with everyone because most people will be intuitive to know when and how to respect your boundaries. Other people will need boundaries clearly defined for them or they won't understand your boundaries or respect them. There is no reason or need for rude, angry, or offensive words when setting boundaries, just state what is needed and desired, or not desired, as clearly and calmly as possible. *Explaining why you are setting a boundary can also help to anchor an expectation, agreement, or desired behavior with another person.*

It is important that boundaries be appropriate and reasonable with fair limits, while not being overly harsh or restrictive. Overly harsh or restrictive boundaries are hurtful and can damage a relationship irreparably. When you create rigid or constrictive rules in relationships, rather than fair and reasonable boundaries, these additional considerations require energy to implement and energy to adhere to and sustain. Avoid rules if possible, as these cloud relationships and add more burden requiring unnecessary expended energy. Utilize agreements rather than rules, as agreements bring both people into a position of compromised equality.

There are people who will want to set boundaries with you, but who will avoid allowing you to set boundaries with them, or respect the boundaries you have set. Consideration must always be given to insure the agreed upon boundaries are reasonable, fair, and reciprocal between the parties involved.

You will encounter those who have few boundaries regarding privacy and openly share information about everything in their lives and everyone else's lives, whereas other people are private and share limited information about their lives. Either approach to personal privacy boundaries is fine. Learn to respect the privacy of the people who are more private and to be open when you feel trusted and trusting. Because a person is open and forthcoming, it does not mean everyone they engage, including you, will be or is at the same level of openness. When people lack healthy boundaries or lack respect for boundaries, you are not obligated to limit or let down your boundaries. When we set healthy and respectful boundaries for ourselves and with others, we move into a space of taking personal responsibility for our needs and desires as *Adults*, ultimately maintaining long-term relationships that mutually serve our collective ever changing needs.

Setting Boundaries

What are some of the signs of needed boundaries? Failed commitments, failed agreements, unfulfilled expectations, verbally abusive words, intrusive behavior, privacy issues, and over-commitment of your time, energy, or personal resources. The following are examples of boundaries we might set for ourselves and with others:

Keeping commitments for when and what time you are to meet or get together.

Keeping confidences, confidential or private information.

Fair sharing of financial costs for shared events or shared space.

Setting a boundary with a person who wants to control how, when, or what you do in your personal life.

Friends wanting to cross into romantic or sexual relationships when the mutual feeling of attraction is not there.

Parents wanting to control every decision in one's adult life.

If the setting of healthy boundaries has been missing in your relationships, then learning to set healthy boundaries will seem uncomfortable at first, and the new behavior may seem unexpected or even offensive to those around you. However, not setting clear boundaries leads to giving too much, being used, or taken advantage of. Boundaries used to control or manipulate another person's behavior are also unfair and unreasonable. A fine line is continually observed between setting boundaries for personal resources and setting inhibiting boundaries or boundaries used to manipulate or control the relationship.

Being clear about how you ask for what you need is important in setting boundaries and removes ambiguity. As an example, instead of asking, "Can you do _____ for me?" it might be better to ask, "Would you do _____ for me?" The former question is asking if someone is capable of an action. The latter question asks directly is they will perform the action.

If your tendency is to give away your resources too freely, then resolving to set needed personal boundaries will change people's responses to you and the dynamics of your relationships. Some people will understand and become more reciprocal in their giving and taking. Others will not respond well, which tells you they come from a non-reciprocal place of expecting only to receive. You may also get the response: "Well, I would do it for *you.*" This is the response from someone who primarily takes, and so it becomes important to look at the context, the length of the relationship, and the person's past behavior to see if the facts support the statement, and if they would in fact *do it for you.* Only you can decide what feels truthful. People who make this statement are usually the ones who ask too much of other people, or try to manipulate people to get what they want.

When a person sets a boundary, honor it, and expect that person to respect your boundaries as well. When boundaries are set and then ignored, a lack of respect, passive aggressive behavior, or invasive behavior is indicated. When boundaries are transgressed or crossed inappropriately, new boundaries may be needed to resolve the resulting conflict. Broken boundaries or boundaries not respected can erode the trust in the relationship and diminish the ability to engage in greater intimacy. If you have to repeatedly set the same boundaries or new boundaries, stop and take the time to reconsider the relationship. If you value the relationship enough to keep it, then ask one final time for respect of your boundaries, and be clear that this is your last time to ask. If the individual continues to cross fair and reasonable boundaries and be disrespectful of your wishes, then it may be time to let go of the relationship in its current form.

Your body and personal space also require setting boundaries. Appropriate touch of your body and the physical distance you prefer to maintain are your boundaries to claim. People who are overly affectionate, overly physical, or are invasive to your private space may need boundaries set for what is appropriate contact, depending on the type of relationship.

When it comes to your neighbors, good boundaries make for good neighbors. A good neighbor respects boundaries and will come tell you when there is a problem before making a small problem a bigger problem. Becoming good citizens as *Adults* requires that we set and respect fair and reasonable boundaries.

When Yes Means Yes and No Means No

Anyone can ask anything of you, at any time, and developing the ability to clearly state *yes* or *no* is one of our healthiest boundaries. This could include people you know, people who are strangers, or people who come in and out of your life temporarily. Anytime you say *no*, you are setting a boundary. Saying *yes* can be a clear removal of boundaries. When requests align with personal intentions or desires, people are comfortable with saying *yes*. Learning to say *no* to requests is often much more difficult. *No* is often perceived as rejection or as overly harsh, but usually it is only harsh if the person receiving the *no* interprets it harshly or as rejection. A clear *no* delivered calmly and assertively is neither harsh, nor rejecting.

Yes is often used to avoid conflicts and to please the needs of other people, and often when we are really feeling we want to say *no*. Using *no* as a means of setting clear boundaries clears up ambiguity in our relationships. When we learn to clearly say *no,* we become much clearer about when we want to say *yes*. Saying *no* with conviction does not give people any room to come back and ask again, or to negotiate to get a *yes*. *No* means no. People may project unhealthy feelings onto you, such as guilt or shame, because they are not getting what they want from you. This is another form of manipulation that is based in un-adult behavior.

What you are for and what you are against defines who you are. Your affirmations and convictions give your life direction and purpose. When you say *no*, be conscious as to why you are saying *no*, because a *no* answer has finality to it, and under different circumstances or at a later time you may wish you had said *yes*. Also, you can say *no*, and then offer a caveat to help find a solution that will elicit an eventual *yes*. Including a caveat creates a collaborative process of finding a solution to a request that is either not possible or requires assistance to achieve.

Indecisiveness and ambiguity often occur because people cannot be decisive about their desires or what is true for them. Get clear on your feelings, then say *yes* or *no* according to what is true for you or desired, and move on. Others, of course, have the same right. You do not always have to say *yes* to be liked or loved. The most courteous and polite response is to tell the person why you are not willing to grant a request, so they can understand where you are coming from. You don't have to provide this last step of justification if this does not apply or is not your preference, but it is courteous to provide a reason for further understanding or when an explanation is requested. Healthy *Adults* ask for what they want and are not afraid of getting or giving *no* for an answer. Receiving a *no* can also be a gentle reminder to our egos that we are not always the center of the universe. Healthy *Adults* are able to accept *no* without personalizing the answer as something negative about them.

You can care and be concerned for another's feelings, but you can never be totally responsible for another's feelings, especially when there is no mal-intent or desire on your part to hurt another in an interaction. An *Adult* understands he or she may make requests of other people during their lives, and those people may not be able or willing to fulfill the requests. A fact of life is this: We don't always get from others or from life what we want or what we expect. Over the course of one's existence, life will say *yes* to us many times, and life may say *no* just as much. Learning when and how to accept either answer will be one of life's great challenges. Many great people who achieved their visions, successes, or new ideas were told *no* many times and persevered because they believed in themselves and in their ability to stay the course.

We can find ourselves pulled into other people's emergencies, ambiguous engagements, or other life dramas, and clear boundaries of *yes* and *no* are needed to maintain one's own peace and happiness. When an emergency is presented to you, the questions to ask yourself are: Is the situation a true emergency? Is this an emergency for which you can actually provide some form of help? Is the emergency some form of life drama you are being pulled into? Are you being asked to rescue people because of bad choices or decisions they have made? Are you being asked to do something that they can do for themselves? The emergencies of others do not have to become your emergencies unless they are true emergencies, and you have the resources to help. Recognize when there is a true emergency, and when you are being pulled into a drama or dysfunctional relationship to accommodate another person's immediate needs in an unnecessary or unhealthy way. Emergencies require empathy and awareness to decide with each circumstance presented how to proceed.

There will be people in our lives who overstep in certain areas or take advantage of our kindness that need clear boundaries set. If you are asked to be untruthful to another person, to deceive another in any way, or to harm another person or creature, you have the right to say *no* based purely on the principle that it is inappropriate to request these behaviors from another person. You have the right to say *no* to people who intentionally use up your time or your resources for their own benefit, or advantage.

There are people who have great difficulty saying *no*. In extreme cases, such people are known as people pleasers, people without clear boundaries who are unable to say *no* to anyone. They often create turmoil for themselves and for others because they cannot state *yes* for what they truly desire or *no* for what they do not desire. Their inability can lead to feelings of resentment or failed commitments in their relationships because their desires are unknown or misunderstood, or they continually over-commit their personal resources. Some people pleasers apologize excessively because they have low self-esteem, or have no idea how to resolve conflicts. Continually apologizing is used to navigate past, present, or perceived conflicts or transgressions. An apology is in order if you have failed to meet one or more of your responsibilities. If you've done nothing to hurt another's feelings, no apology is needed.

133

People are often afraid to say *no* in order to avoid conflict or because of the negative connotations associated with the word *no*. When you say *no* to another person, and they get angry or upset, it usually means the individual is personalizing the boundary of *no*, or considers their needs more important than yours. It can also mean the intent is not in your best interest or mutual best interest and is potentially selfish or self-serving.

You are also not responsible for another's responses or feelings when you say *no*. Are anyone's needs more important than yours when it comes to requests for your time and personal resources? Getting a clear response, either a *yes* or a *no*, sets a clear boundary with no ambiguity and gives everyone involved a clear direction for how to proceed. While *yes* is more affirming, both *yes* and *no* are always possible outcomes to requests, and equally valid.

Privacy

The need for personal privacy (differing from solitude or personal space) is another aspect of personal boundaries necessary as long as judgmentalism exists. This includes the safeguarding of personal or private information. Respect for another's privacy and your personal privacy is required in healthy *Adult* relationships. When private information is used to judge another, rather than an unconditional acceptance of the imperfections of our humanity, it causes separation and harm. Without the tendency to judge one another, there would be no need for privacy and no need for private information.

Our usual privacy concerns revolve around our relationships with others, including our sexual relationships, sexuality, money, work, financial matters, spiritual beliefs or religion, mental or physical health, age and politics. Often there are personal preferences we wish to remain private, except in our closest intimate relationships. One's personal life or privacy concerns are no one else's business unless one chooses to share them.

A person who does not have good filters or relays too much private information too quickly is probably not a person who can be trusted to respect confidential agreements or privacy with others. Learning to discern who has appropriate filters and respect for privacy in your personal relationships will serve you well. Also, asking or being asked personal questions without a previously established personal relationship or the corresponding intimacy is invasive. Our level of personal disclosure is directly relative to the amount of trust we have with the person receiving the information. At times, privacy can be required because a person is not capable of understanding the reason for the privacy or the ramifications of disclosure.

Secrets are often confused with privacy. Secrets are agreements to keep information confidential. Privacy relates to the areas of one's life considered private with no need for disclosure or discussion. Information that you want to remain completely private is best not told to anyone. People can make requests for any information from you, but you always have the right to simply answer, "That is personal or private information I would rather not share." Even when you decide to share your personal information, you have the right to choose when and with whom you share. There is a tendency to feel obligated to answer any question from anybody, even complete strangers. In actuality there is never any obligation to answer private or intimate questions until the relationship has naturally evolved to a level of intimacy and trust that warrants private disclosures. If there is information you want to remain personal and confidential, the only true guarantee that it will remain private is not to disclose it at all.

Containment is the ability to keep private or personal information confidential. Everything personal does not need disclosure, although today's societies often invade the privacy of famous and even not so famous people. Personal energy is conserved when we retain private and personal information, or there is no desire to disclose to others information that we wish to contain. *Containment* is particularly important regarding disclosure of personal health information, financial information, relationship problems, and sexual or emotional intimacy with others. These are topics best discussed

135

with the person directly involved, with the closest of friends or family and not in mixed company or with casual acquaintances.

Too often private information is made public without a person's consent. One way this occurs is through disclosure by association, when people make assumptions about others because of information they acquire about a friend or spouse. Disclosure by association occurs when personal information is shared about acquaintances and then is assumed to also apply to those with whom they are engaged in relationship. Privacy is maintained and respected when these types of assumptions are ignored and not entertained.

People can be overly curious about all aspects of other people's lives with no respect or sensitivity to pick up on the boundaries of others. Set clearer boundaries with overly curious people and engage in interactions in which you provide only the information you are comfortable providing. Often the intent of one's curiosity is not support, love, or care, but rather the obtaining of information to satisfy one's own need to know, to gossip, or to relay the information to someone else.

A note of interest: Languages outside of English have two uses of personal pronouns, one for those people with whom you are familiar and one for those you choose to address more formally. This clear delineation between familiar or formal associations allows for a natural boundary of privacy to exist. In these languages, a person is *invited* to use the more personal and familiar case of the pronoun, and does not use it *until* invited. This creates a boundary through language with a person until trust and respect have developed in the relationship to allow people to become more personally involved and the invitation is extended. Similarly, until there is trust and respect established in a relationship, boundaries and containment are needed for what is discussed and what is not discussed when people cross into inquiry that is too personal about you, about themselves, or about other people. We individually determine when a relationship contains sufficient intimacy for further disclosure.

Our individual relationship dynamics are not collectively additive in nature. Your business is your direct engagement with each individual relationship. We are only personally responsible for our direct relationship with each individual we engage, and not the transitive, indirect, or peripheral relationships that develop between others. Other people's relationships with their friends, family, life partners, sexual partners, dates, extra-marital affairs, divorces, etc., are none of your business. If someone invites you to discuss a private relationship issue, then be a good listener, or give an opinion expressing your support whenever you can, without engaging in gossip or conversation that is negative, unsupportive, or unconstructive. Relationships are hard enough to maintain without the addition of idle gossip or negative comments, which do nothing to serve anyone constructively.

The invasiveness of modern day media has made privacy issues for public people uncomfortable, hurtful, and in some extreme cases deadly. For healthy boundaries with public people, it is better to respect privacy issues of others, no matter how public they are, so their difficult life issues are not up for random scrutiny by the public at large.

For politicians and world leaders, our vote is best cast based on their leadership abilities, without concerning ourselves with their personal lives as long as they are law-abiding citizens, and their words are consistent with their actions. Voting is a right in most countries to allow democracy to unfold, not to expose personal lives. We all go through difficult times and challenging situations in our lives, so do not judge another unless you can clearly state your slate is clean. No one would want their difficult times to become public. In addition, the lives of others are not that interesting when one's own life has the proper focus and direction without the distraction of such pettiness.

We are entitled to know when our private information, buying habits, or personal preferences are being sold, used to market to us, or used to manipulate us to buy goods or services. Gathering of our personal data can be used constructively or destructively depending on its application.

Money and financial issues are your private information with limited need for disclosure, as doing so can lead to jealousy, resentment, or expectations around money that are unreasonable or unfair. An example might be those perceived to have more money should always pay, pay more than their fair share or have no need to receive gifts from others. Everyone should pay their fair share and nothing more in whatever way they can. Others may use financial information to judge a person's status or overall value, which is not a fair basis upon which to judge a person, ever. Telling someone how much you make in salary, how much money you have, or what you paid for something is also not necessary and usually carries negative consequences. For example, you get a substantial raise at work, and you tell close friends or family about your raise and how substantial it was. You may find they change how they deal with you and expect you to pay more or take on more financial responsibility just because you have a raise, while you might need to save the money for your retirement, a much deserved acquisition, or desire to apply it to a child's college fund. Whatever information it is used for, your private information is yours and no one else's business. No one needs to know how much money you make, how much you have, how much you own, or any other information related to your personal property or financial situation, and learning to keep this information private is important.

Regarding physical and mental health issues, each person approaches their personal health issues differently, from disclosing everything to being extremely private. Either way is a personal choice each of us must make and then mutually respect. Many governments have adopted privacy laws so people are neither discriminated against nor refused public services because of health or handicap issues. People with disabilities and handicaps require our compassion and special consideration, not our judgment or discrimination.

If a person has health-related issues or sexually transmitted diseases, these are best discussed with one's health professionals, potential sexual partners, or with the people who they have chosen to share this information. Beyond this, these issues are not the concern or business of others. It is hard to know when talking about someone's illness will hurt them or somebody else involved with them, and for this reason more caution and discretion should be used when discussing the private health-related issues of anyone.

Finally, political positions and views can be personal and emotionally charged. These are best kept private unless those present are open to a respectful discussion or share similar political ideas. Any political debate should be based on truth and facts, so everyone comes away better informed.

Each person has the right to disclosure or privacy of their sexual preference. It is inappropriate to ask a person their sexual preference unless the question is meant to communicate that you are interested in them sexually. Questions about sexuality can put a person in an uncomfortable position, especially if they are unsure or undecided. Too often people ask these kinds of question for their own personal knowledge or to share the knowledge through gossip. A person's sexual preference is no one else's business.

Relationships with people who are overly invasive or lack respect for boundaries or privacy become difficult because your energy becomes consumed by the need to constantly set or reset boundaries. If you know a person gossips, is overly invasive, or cannot keep confidences with you or other people, then set clear boundaries with this individual early on.

All of the privacy issues discussed above require permission for disclosure or discussion. Without this permission, these areas of privacy are to be held in private regard and respected. Maintaining one's own life and personal affairs requires plenty of effort of its own, and it is a waste of time to become involved in the personal affairs of others. Get clear about what comprises your business, their business, and everyone else's business. Of these three, only one is your responsibility or under your control-*your business*. The decision making process for what is your business and under your control is an important lesson in becoming a responsible *Adult*.

Some might argue that privacy is hiding from the truth. If everyone, everywhere, could always accept another's truth without judgment, then privacy would never be required, and truth would always prevail. As previously stated, privacy exists because judgmentalism exists. There is hope for a day in the future when acceptance and non-judgment are the norm, and no one has the need or desire to pass judgment on another, deny another's rights, or place stigma on anyone for anything ever again. Until then, our privacy is needed.

CHAPTER NINE

Drama

Many people talk about drama in relationships and say they do not want to engage in drama, often not fully understanding what drama actually is or its ramifications. However, to stay out of drama it is necessary to understand how to identify drama, and more importantly, how to step out of drama. Just what exactly is drama in relationships?

The Drama Triangle

In his 1968 article, "Fairy Tales and Script Drama Analysis," author Stephen B. Karpman, M.D. identified the three main roles we play in our relationships with others that constitute drama.[6] These three roles are the **P**ersecutor, the **R**escuer and the **V**ictim. Dr. Karpman further illustrated this as "The Drama Triangle," Figure 2.

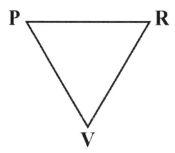

Figure 2: Karpman Drama Triangle

---

[6] Stephen B. Karpman, M.D., The Drama Triangle

http://www.karpmandramatriangle.com/pdf/thenewdramatriangles.pdf

A person steps into the Victim role when he or she wants to be rescued, seeks unnecessary sympathy, or does not want to take responsibility for their life circumstances. The reason a person engages in victim behavior usually centers on a perceived need to be rescued from their past or to elicit help or attention from others. The Victim may want to blame others for their current life condition and thus avoid taking personal responsibility for their own behaviors, actions, or inactions. There is usually no real emergency requiring rescue, but rather some underlying need or ulterior motive at work requiring outside intervention or attention. Playing the role of the Victim may also be a way to avoid contributing responsibly to a given situation. This avoidance is used to ensure that when things go wrong, someone else is at fault.

The role of the Persecutor occurs when a person does not get what they expect or want in an interaction and instead of accepting the outcome, persecutes, punishes, or blames the individual who failed to meet their expectations or desires. A Persecutor may get angry or resentful and react in negative or punishing ways with abusive language or abusive behavior, through the cutting off of resources, or by pulling away from the relationship or terminating it completely.

Finally, the Rescuer wants to help by fixing others, solving their problems, or making decisions for them, even when help is not requested or required. When the rescuer steps in to help, their motives may have other underlying reasons. Some examples might be: "If I help you, then maybe I can change or control you," or, "If I help you, then you will love me."

All three roles may operate from beliefs arising from unresolved childhood issues, such as abandonment, emotional or physical abuse, or emotional neglect. Common to all three roles of the Drama Triangle are ulterior motives at work. Because of this, the behavior of all three respective roles is often controlling or manipulative in some way. People in these roles will try to gain control through anger and guilt tripping. They either get angry with you for what you could have done, or they want to make you feel guilty for what you should have done. Attempting to control others by actively or passively telling them what to do, or how to do it gets tiresome and often creates distance and separation in relationships, not the harmony we all seek.

***

What are the controlling behaviors of the Drama Triangle's three roles?

A Victim controls by repeatedly asking for help and engaging others for their time, energy, or resources. A Persecutor controls through the time and resources they give to others, often metering out rewards and punishment. A Rescuer controls by giving time or resources along with an expectation that these will be repaid, or the Rescuer will be rescued in return. All of the roles have the ulterior motive of controlling another person in some manner or for some purpose.

Some people attempt to control others by not responding to requests to engage, by withholding requested information, or by not providing feedback. Not responding to requests can be a passive/aggressive form of control. A request made by a person you care about is always worthy of a response, even if the response is a simple *no*. Indecision affecting others can also be indicative of passive aggressive behavior.

There will be drama when people engage in playing any of the three roles on the drama triangle. The drama intensifies when there is a shift in roles: a Victim becomes a Persecutor, a Rescuer becomes a Victim, a Persecutor flips into either the Victim or Rescuer roles, or any combination of these three movements. A role can switch to another role at any given time, and when the shift happens, some sort of drama in the relationship usually accompanies it.

The more shifts or roles taking place over time, the more drama will be experienced. For example, when a Victim is not helped or rescued, they can move into the role of Persecutor. When a Rescuer's help or advice is not followed or accepted, their resentment can cause the Rescuer to become a Persecutor. When a Persecutor's behavior is admonished, a flip into the role of Victim can take place. The movements can be subtle or can happen very distinctly in rapid succession.

When a person is entrenched in drama, movement can occur among all three roles in a single interaction. An example: a person (Rescuer) insists on offering help to someone who has not asked for their help; the help is not needed nor is it willingly received. When the Rescuer's help is declined, they get upset, angry and stomp off, abandoning the interaction as a Persecutor. The Persecutor then blames the person who did not accept the help, assumes the role of Victim and accuses the other of ruining their day. Drama may also occur when a person steps out of the Drama Triangle, such as when a Victim is no longer being rescued, and becomes a Persecutor of the person who will no longer rescue them. People may deflect or blame others to avoid taking personal responsibility or accountability for their own behavior.

It always takes at least two people to create drama and a subsequent shift to another drama role, because if one person identifies the drama and does not engage in these behaviors, then the drama cannot take place.

While drama may be entertaining to us when watched on TV, a stage, or on a big movie screen, drama is not fun, entertaining, or healthy when it occurs in real life personal relationships. More often than not, drama is a waste of time and energy causing anguish, sleepless nights, and unnecessary stress. All of the energy used to resolve dramas can instead be used to enjoy life through much more productive endeavors and in the seeking and building of healthier relationships.

The roles of Victim, Persecutor, and Rescuer can also have deeper and unhealthier patterns of behavior. These include the Narcissist or Egoist, the Altruist or Martyr, and the Masochist or Sadist.[7]

---

[7] *While the terms Masochist and Sadist are often used to identify sexual aberrations, these terms are used here to describe extreme behavioral personality traits, and their corresponding behaviors in relationship dynamics.*

Narcissists and Egoists are people who are overly self-obsessed. The Narcissist or Egoist is an extension of the Persecutor role, and these people tend to be concerned only for themselves and the meeting of their own needs, without concern or empathy for the needs of others. They will often engage in relationships to manipulate and control other people to get their needs met. The pure Narcissist is often unaware they think only of themselves, and even when another points out their narcissistic behavior, the feedback usually falls on deaf ears. The typical Narcissist never or rarely meets another's needs, or is even concerned about another's need. A Narcissist usually fails to offer support, and if the focus or attention is on someone else, they attempt to divert focus and attention back to themselves through some personal drama or created need. The Narcissist wants to be the center of attention, and can act out negatively or in a punishing manner when their needs are not met or the attention they desire is not gained.

The Narcissist with a large enough ego becomes an Egoist. The Egoist not only serves their own needs, but they think they are always right and may feel completely justified in their purely self-serving behaviors and beliefs. Egoists often exhibit controlling or manipulative behaviors as well. Ostracization or revenge can occur when the Narcissist or Egoist no longer receives the attention they desire or are no longer able to manipulate or maintain control over a personal relationship.

Narcissists or Egoists may occasionally do something for others, but only as a means to draw attention to themselves or eventually get their own personal needs met, either directly or indirectly. Their needs are most important and take precedence over everything and everyone. They often take way more than they are willing to give. Egoists control others through their constant need for attention and making everyone around them feel obligated and subservient to those needs. A relationship with an Egoist requiring subservience is akin to slavery. When involved with an Egoist, you will spend all of your time meeting their needs, and rarely is there reciprocity, regard or return of consideration.

Extensions of the Victim role include the Altruists or Martyrs. Altruists are people who are overly obsessed with pleasing others. The pure Altruist can be an extension of either the Rescuer role or the Victim role, depending on if the person wants to rescue others or desires rescuing by others. The Altruist is constantly doing things for other people, giving things, or taking care of others, often at the expense of taking care of their own needs. Instead of coming from a place of giving only when and what is needed, the Altruist gives with either a conscious or unconscious expectation for something in return. Altruists often give to other people with the expectation of a payback such as love, a return gift, or similar displays of affection or behavior. Usually these expectations center on wanting to be liked or the need for affection or love, but some Altruists may even expect financial returns for their "gifts" or care.

The extreme Altruist becomes a Martyr when all of their giving is done with a conscious or unconscious intention to suffer, so they can then be recognized for their sacrifice or suffering and be rescued or given to in return. This suffering is the Martyr's general approach to life, usually accompanied by a story line of: "Look at all I have done for you!"

A Martyr takes on more than they can handle without asking for or accepting help, and then when they get in over their heads and finally do ask for help and no one is available, they get to play the Victim. The Rescuer Altruist gets the perceived payoff of being recognized as the selfless Martyr because of all they have done for the person or people being rescued. The Rescuer will eventually assume feelings of resentment if their over-giving or rescuing behavior is not acknowledged or reciprocated in some form.

Another aspect of the Altruist is people pleasing or trying to make other people happy. Altruists try to please everyone in their lives at all times. None of us can please everyone in our lives, nor do we always have the resources. At some point we discover no one else can make anyone else happy, nor should anyone want that responsibility. The only person's happiness you have control over is your own. We cannot be in charge of other people's happiness,

146

and it is a form of arrogance to believe we can make another person happy or make decisions for others that will bring them happiness. All we can do is provide our gifts of joy and personal resources to others, and then allow them to choose how or if they will receive our gifts.

The people pleasing behavior of Altruists can become a problem in relationships for various reasons. People-pleasers can become exhausted, as they often spread themselves so thin in their desire to please others, they cannot give the proper attention and care to the people and relationships that matter most in their lives. They can then enact the Victim role through their disappointment in themselves. When a person is striving to please too many people, assigning no priority to the people who really matter, their loved ones may conclude they are of little or no importance. Setting clear priorities for those who are important and learning how to be in a relationship where the basis is not just pleasing behavior, helps to relieve the people pleaser of their constant need to please.

A Rescuer or Victim may find themselves in the role of people-pleasing, but for different reasons. The Rescuer wants to keep everyone happy, often to avoid conflict, and the Victim attempts to win acceptance and love by pleasing others. Questions to ask the people pleaser include: "Can you really make another person happy?" "Are you responsible for another's happiness?" "Will my words or actions truly make others happy?" When we stop and are honest in answering these questions, we often find trying to make anyone, other than ourselves happy is usually a waste of time, money, and energy. We all have to find happiness for ourselves, and our paths to happiness belong to each one of us to discover. You can certainly provide your gifts and support to another person in their quest to find happiness, but you cannot do the work for them, or provide the state of happiness for them.

Contrary to people pleasing are the extreme behaviors of self-deprecation and persecution that occur when the Persecutor or Victim shifts to the extreme roles of the Sadist or Masochist. The Masochist may enjoy persecution by others, or seek out persecuting behaviors from others. In

147

addition to enjoying persecuting behaviors, the Masochist may also enjoy the attention that is obtained by continually setting themselves up for failure. A Sadist not only persecutes others but also may seek to persecute others when their expectations fail or requests are denied, often for no known reason or unfairly. The Sadist not only seeks to persecute others, but also gets enjoyment from persecuting others and making them suffer.

As seen above, the roles of drama can range from subtle to extreme, but drama at any level or in any form takes energy from us and diminishes enjoyment of our relationships. Getting out of the drama in your relationships gives you back the energy you have been exerting to continually maintain the drama. Getting out of the drama allows you to put your life back into perspective and to reutilize the energy you reclaim from drama for engaging with others in fulfilling dynamic relationships based on constructive and healthy behaviors. There is a healthier way to engage in relationship, and that way occurs when we interact through The Healthy Triangle.

The Healthy Triangle

There is a healthy version of the Drama Triangle exhibiting self-awareness and self-responsibility while taking us out of drama and into healthy Adult roles. The three healthy roles presented in the Healthy Triangle are: Decisive, Empathetic, and Vulnerable.

In healthy relationships, the Victim becomes a person of Vulnerability who is in a position of needing help for actual hardship or loss. The healthy version of the Persecutor role embodies the quality of constructive Decisiveness and confidently expresses what they desire from others. And finally, the healthy version of the Rescuer role is someone who has the capacity for Empathy and understands when and how to help others. The Healthy Triangle is shown in Figure 3.

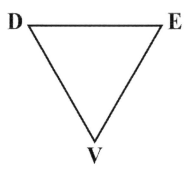

Figure 3: The Healthy Triangle[89]

Those in the category of Vulnerable are usually experiencing a challenging but temporary life experience requiring the help, support, or assistance of others. This could have to do with the loss of a loved one, the loss of a job, a divorce, a serious medical diagnosis; or other situations serious enough to affect the person's joy, productivity, or life situation. A person in the Vulnerable position does what he or she can to deal with their life circumstances, asking for help for what they do not know or cannot do for themselves. Their primary intent is to do all they can to solve their own problems and to help themselves as much as possible. Once these possibilities are exhausted, they then ask for help when outside help is truly needed. The Vulnerable person is able to ask for help without negative emotions or punishing others when their needs are not met. Healthy statements from a person in the position of Vulnerability may be: "I need your help and support during this time. Would you help me by doing _____?" or "I don't need you to solve my problem, but I could use your help in figuring out a solution."

When someone is going through a hard time, loss, a disappointment, or an illness, then offering our help, support, or consolation in any way we can

---

[8] Susan Eldridge LCSW, 'The Healthy Triangle', Whitepaper, 2010

[9] Acey Choy, "The Winner's Triangle", Transactional Analysis Journal Vol.20 (1) January 1990 pp40-46;

is appropriate. Sometimes your care and support is all you can offer a person who is in a vulnerable position, and other times may require personal resources that you provide to assist them. No one can do emotional healing for another person, but we can offer our care, support, and guidance if these are welcomed.

A person in a vulnerable state must also be careful that people who do offer help have no ulterior motives or attached expectations. Another way of indebting or controlling others can be through offers of assistance during times of vulnerability. It must be clear that the help being offered will actually *be* helpful and not just a token for the express purpose of reward or recognition so the person giving help can feel better about themselves.

The Decisive person is one who knows what they want for themselves and is able to state their desires in a confident, non-threatening, non-controlling, and non-punishing way. The primary motive and intent of the Decisive person is to clearly state their needs, wants, or desires without expression of negative emotions or an unhealthy attachment to the outcome. The Decisive person does not punish others when their needs are not met.

Decisive people are also able to set clear boundaries with others for what they need and desire from others and in their relationships. Their needs and desires are presented with a consideration to the needs and desires of others. When a Decisive person is wronged by another or needs to set a boundary, they are able to calmly and clearly state their needs for the situation without going into the role of Persecutor.

A Decisive person may be perceived as aggressive in our current society. In reality Decisive people are usually able to articulate directly what they want for themselves without diffusive language or ambiguity. This clarity and directness has the effect of lessening misunderstandings and removing ambiguity in relationships. Using directness when needed is a healthy approach to Adult living and represents healthy Adult behavior. Decisive people understand their needs are not necessarily the concerns of others nor can others always grant their needs, but they have learned to clearly state what they desire and what they need from others. They understand their requests may be granted or possibly denied, and they are accepting of these as potential outcomes.

The Empathetic person is someone who recognizes the needs of others and can be there for them when they are vulnerable or truly need assistance, without being manipulated or used by other people to get their time, money, energy, love, or care. The Empathetic person is able to discern when others can do what is needed to take care of themselves, when help is actually needed, and when they can provide help. The primary motive or intent of a healthy Empathetic person is this: "Don't do for others what they can do for themselves," or, "Don't do for others what you haven't been asked to do." A healthy person in a vulnerable position who needs help will ask for help. You can be compassionate and offer to help a person who is unable to ask for help, doesn't know how to ask for help, or who doesn't know what help is needed. The vulnerable person being offered help is then allowed to choose whether or not they want to accept the help offered without any repercussions or unwanted conditions.

Advice is a gift of ideas or thoughts given freely without attachment to the outcome. Offering guidance, direction, or knowledge is generous and kind, but others are not always open to accepting it or do not understand the gift of what is being offered. The simple rule for advice is: Avoid offering unsolicited advice to those who have not asked for your advice or help. When there is no gratitude for advice or help offered, this also confirms your advice and help were not requested or welcome. If you are asked for your help or opinion, preface the help you offer by stating that they can take your advice and act on it or not. They are free to choose to use your advice, or decline it, as they desire. If the help or advice offered has an attached expectation that it be done a certain way, this could be the controlling behavior of a Rescuer with associated motives. If this is the case, then both parties step back into the Drama Triangle as Rescuer and Victim.

151

The Healthy Triangle roles of Empathetic, Vulnerable, and Decisive replace the unhealthy roles found in the Drama Triangle of Rescuer, Victim and Persecutor thus taking us out of drama and the need for drama, and into healthy and sustaining Adult behaviors. Identifying the drama is the first step in movement out of the unhealthy behaviors of the drama triangle.

Identifying the Drama

Raising your awareness of drama by understanding the roles of the Drama Triangle and the roles of the Healthy Triangle is key to stepping out of drama in your relationships. You will eventually develop the awareness to recognize the preliminary signs of drama behaviors by yourself and others, and you will be able to extricate yourself from this behavior before you are entangled in the fray. An awareness of drama and the roles we play allows us to step back and choose not to engage in the drama and not to engage in unhealthy roles when we develop the self-awareness to recognize them at their onset or during their enactment. This is the critical first step. Your awareness and understanding of the roles and how you engage in them is key to learning how to step out of them. You become fully aware of your own motives, behaviors, and involvement in any drama and how they map to the three roles of Victim, Rescuer, and Persecutor. From this awareness, you can then become aware of which role or roles you naturally gravitate toward and enact when drama is presented.

The motives we bring to the creation of unhealthy drama can be subtle, but learning to identify when a person is playing a given drama role, or when we are being pulled into a given drama role, is an important first step toward moving out of these patterns of behavior.

One way to do this is to become aware of unnecessary emotional noise in your life. Unnecessary emotional noise is any emotional upset occurring when there are un-realized, unrealistic, or unfulfilled expectations. Emotional

152

noise usually occurs when there is a shift from one drama role to another, such as when a Victim does not get their needs met and becomes a Persecutor.

The roles on the Drama Triangle always lead to dysfunctional behavior in relationships, and often the people playing the roles are either unaware or in denial of the behavior. All of the roles may involve a life script being played out repeatedly by oneself or the other person. Recognition of these patterns helps one in this first step of awareness to eventually move out of these unhealthy patterns of behavior completely.

After awareness is established, the second step is taking full responsibility for the actions and behaviors that contributed to your role in the drama, and healing the underlying causes that brought you to engage in the drama in the first place. Getting clear ownership for our part in any unhealthy and unnecessary drama in relationships allows us to get clearer on the patterns within ourselves that lead to dysfunctional relationships. If you observe yourself and others carefully, you will start to see the recurring roles of Victim, Rescuer or Persecutor at play. Observation is critical to identifying and stepping out of drama.

The third step is to set healthy boundaries by limiting or removing your involvement in the drama or limiting your engagement with those who regularly want to engage you in drama. Setting boundaries can be everything from saying *no* when you are being asked to participate in drama, or *no* to behaviors that pull you into one of the roles on the Drama Triangle. Your goal will be to develop more skill in becoming self-aware of drama and stepping out of the pattern by setting clear boundaries at the onset, rather than later as the drama unfolds, or at its unhealthy conclusion. The best approach with those who engage drama is to set up parameters for how to interact such as limiting the time spent with those involved in drama, or asking for their participation to not bring drama into your interactions. Examples include meeting in public places or neutral locations that allow easy exit when there is drama, or driving two cars rather than being a captive audience to the drama in one car. Learning to set boundaries early on when drama emerges is critical to stepping out of drama.

The fourth step is to recognize the simple fact that one cannot change another person or that person's behavior, but one can change the response to another's behavior. In effect, the only thing we can change is our words, actions, and behaviors in response to a person engaged in drama or trying to engage us in drama. A person will only change when they are aware that change is needed and they are ready and willing to make changes. It is each person's responsibility to make personal changes, but it is not your responsibility to tell them they need to change or how to change. Instead of jumping in and offering help or advice to others, you might take the first step by asking them if they would like your help or advice. When you take this important first step in helping another, you show them you respect them enough to ask for their permission, and by doing this you don't waste your time and energy providing help or advice that is unwelcome. Stepping in and providing all of the answers in the hope of solving another's problems may actually stop the learning process they need to experience or the life lessons they need to learn. While we cannot change another person, we can plant seeds and ask questions helping them to see a more truthful approach to life, if they are open and willing for change to occur.

Gradually you will become more aware of when you are being pulled into drama, including what it feels like, looks like, and smells like, and then how to step back and choose another path. No one else is responsible for your thoughts, behaviors, choices, or actions in each moment, and you become an Adult when you learn to take full responsibility for yourself, for your life, and for how you respond to unhealthy patterns of behavior.

Another facet of becoming a responsible Adult is learning to choose an appropriate response, rather than reacting too quickly and over-reacting or responding inappropriately to the situation presented to you. If possible, respond in the moment, but delaying a response to take the time to formulate a thoughtful response can be just as effective. Part of this responsibility always includes the action of apologizing when your thoughts, words, or behaviors are hurtful, manipulative, or abusive. The inaction of not making clear decisions to move forward in a direction to resolve issues is another form of the Victim role, particularly when this inaction is used to stay in unhealthy patterns of behavior, and other people are asked to continue to support the continued patterns of unhealthy or destructive behaviors.

You deserve to engage in healthy, constructive relationships that support and nurture your well-being. Drama takes your time, energy, and emotional health to maintain, and prevents you from living your life to its fullest capability. The only way to step out of the drama is to take responsibility for your words, actions, and behaviors, and any resultant outcomes from these, and then choose to engage differently. We cannot change another person or the roles they choose to play, but we can change the role *we* choose to play, and step out of melodrama.

Engaging in a relationship with a belief that you can change the other person is using an approach that often comes from the roles of Rescuer or Persecutor. If you feel a person needs to change, then you are bringing a judgment of them to the relationship, which has a corresponding premise that you do not accept them as they are. You can accept a person as is, along with a decision not to condone or tolerate unhealthy behaviors. However, no one we interact with can be everything to us or provide everything we need at all times in our relationships. Accept a person as he or she is. Then decide how and if you will interact with that individual based on the person who exists right now, not some fictitious construct of how they might be in the future. We all gain personal freedom when we accept people as they are without the need to change them, and take personal responsibility for our engagement in healthy behaviors.

Getting Out of the Drama

We have identified the three drama roles; now let's look at each one in turn and how we can start to change our behaviors and relationship to others. Relationships cannot be healthy if the basis for engagement rests consistently on any of the dysfunctional behaviors found in drama roles. The Victim will need clear boundaries set for asking or accepting help from others. Victims must stop validating their self-worth by allowing people to use them, help them, or by setting themselves up for rescue by others. The Victim learns to do for themselves and asks for help only when help is truly needed.

The Rescuer will need boundaries set by others for unwanted help they may offer. The Rescuer must realize that it is not possible to save everyone, nor are the gifts of rescue always welcome or needed. The Rescuer must learn to identify internal boundaries for what resources they are willing to give, and only give their resources when they are truly needed, directly requested, and they have them to give.

The Persecutor will need to have clear boundaries set by others for inappropriate controlling or persecuting behaviors. A persecutor must learn to set internal boundaries when they persecute others by realizing their equality and removing the Persecutor's perceived responsibility or position to judge, correct, admonish, or punish others.

The Victim is caught in a thought or belief from some past hurt or trauma, either real or perceived, which causes them to operate in the world from the perspective of being wounded and/or suffering in some way. For a Victim to step out of this role, they must let go of the belief holding them captive to their behavior pattern of dependency on others, needing to be rescued, or allowing others to persecute them. The Victim's motto becomes "I am responsible for myself and can take care of my own needs." "I ask for help from others only when help is truly needed." Once the Victim takes this step to see the hurt or belief that connects them to the Victim pattern, they can start to take full responsibility for their life immediately, forgiving their past and past Persecutors and making better conscious choices going forward. This means the Victim does not get the payback of blaming the world or anyone else for their life condition any longer. Nor does the Victim need to continue their repeated cries for help or search for someone to rescue them. A victim can shift to the rescuer role when they engage in projection of their own need to be rescued by trying to rescue other people.

How do you step out of the Rescuer role? One guideline for a Rescuer is to *stop doing for others what they can do for themselves*. Rescuers often help others because they want to fix them, save them, be liked or loved. It is not their place to become a martyr, a fixer, or the one who rescues, unless a person specifically asks for help and has done everything possible already to meet their own needs or help themselves. Rescuers love being needed, because then they can seek out and rescue those in need and feel valued and worthy through their rescuing behavior. Often a Rescuer is rescuing because they have been abandoned at some key point in their life, so they busy themselves rescuing others when in reality they may be striving to be rescued themselves. Their rescuing of another may actually be a projection of their own need for rescue. Rather than looking inward at their own problems, a rescuer may want to help other people to avoid looking honestly at their own problems. This outward projection keeps them engaged with other's problems without having to look at their own. Rescuing behavior often involves not allowing a person to go through what they need to experience, be it bad or good. The Rescuer wants to "fix" the other person. This is a form of arrogance on the part of the Rescuer. Some of our toughest times can teach us some of our greatest lessons. Why does anyone feel they know what is the right, wrong, good or bad experience for anyone else? You can show support and love when a person is going through a difficult time or making poor choices, without employing rescuing behaviors, such as showing them the way, how to do it, making decisions for them, or taking on solving their problems.

Sometimes just letting a person know you are there with your support is the best help while keeping you out of rescuing behaviors. Don't get involved in managing the lives of others unless they invite you to do so, and even then use caution and restraint. If you step in to rescue someone with your

157

resources, take the time to understand if your resources will actually help the person solve the existing problem or will enable the individual in some way. A person who genuinely needs help will ask for help in figuring out how to solve their problems, not ask you to do the actual solving of the problems. Expecting other people to read your mind to figure out what you need, or trying to read the mind of others to know what they need are other common behaviors of a Victim or Rescuer.

Victims may also play the "I don't have any money" card to get others to step in and pay their way. Financial concerns are often related to poor money management or not living within one's financial means. Offering to pay a person's way is another rescuing behavior taking both financial and emotional energy, and at some point the question becomes "When does it stop?" Is the money being provided just enabling more bad financial decisions and postponing an inevitable financial collapse? Donating your time, money, or other resources to a Victim's call for help often ends up enabling that person to continue creating the same problems. Your resources are used to provide a temporary relief enabling them to stay stuck in problems longer. If you are a Victim, then learn to release the need to be saved and take full responsibility for past, present, and future decisions.

How do you step out of the Persecutor role? The Persecutor gets angry, lashes out, and judges or punishes, because of an emotional hurt from the past or unfulfilled expectations. The Persecutor must learn to recognize the source of this deep pain and heal this first. The second step is to realize that we may make requests of others or have expectations of others, but this does not mean they can or will fulfill our desires or expectations. We do not always get our way, nor is it always about us. And when we don't get our way, feelings of disappointment are a normal response. Persecuting behavior is not a healthy response.

When life doesn't meet our expectations, we cannot allow that one area of life that is not going well to affect the other areas that are going well. Additionally, no one has the right to attack, get angry, judge, lash out, or

158

punish another person in any way when one's expectations are not met. A Persecutor may hold other people to particular standards of behavior or conduct while allowing themselves complete freedom in these same areas. This double standard allows the Persecutor control over another's behavior, while providing themselves the freedom to behave as they please. Once a precedence or standard is set, both people are to adhere to the same standard, not just one. Double standards betray trust in relationships and are best pointed out each time they occur. To heal this pattern of behavior, the Persecutor is to observe their feelings and responses when they step into the Persecutor role, mapping them back to past hurts if these are known, allowing understanding and healing of the source to occur.

People tend to get into problems with another person when one person has needs the other is not able to fulfill. Sometimes this arises because both people are in a place of needing something from the other, yet neither has the energy to provide the other with what they need, so there can be frustration, anger, and conflict because neither person is getting what they need from the relationship. It is important for one or both people to step back and see this happening, and then have a conversation to address the simple fact that neither person is in a place to give willingly to the other, and together find an acceptable solution for the situation. Managing expectations are explored in more depth in Chapter Eleven.

When you begin to step out of the roles of the Drama Triangle, there is a period of renegotiating your relationships that contain the elements of drama. People may see your new behavior as foreign and unusual and may mistake your unwillingness to engage in the drama as aggressive, passive aggressive, or misinterpret your compassion for weakness. Being kind or flexible does not mean a person is weak or doesn't know what they want for themselves. Kind people can also be strong, confident, and direct.

When you change your role and behaviors to something more positive, your new behavior may not be understood. You might try explaining to the people in your life, particularly those people who are playing a corresponding drama role that you desire a healthier relationship, and ask if they are willing to participate in healthier behavior. If they are willing to listen, be clear with them you have assumed an unhealthy role in your relationship with them, what role you have played, and how you plan to change your unhealthy behavior and its unhealthy consequences. Most people won't readily understand until they see your behavioral changes in action, and then you will have to proceed based on their reactions. If they are ready for an *Adult* relationship, then the relationship will go forward on the new terms of healthier behaviors.

The Drama Triangle provides the basis for a common language in how to handle the unhealthy relational dynamics of Rescuer, Victim, and Persecutor. If the ego is too big or operates from a premise that it has all the answers, then understanding the roles in the drama will not be accepted or understood. If people are not ready for healthy *Adult* relationships, then their adverse reaction to you stepping out of the drama will give you this information. The important thing to remember when negative reactions to your desire to change the drama patterns arise is to take time before responding rather than reacting with a response that is angry or punishing, putting you right back into the Drama Triangle again. A mature *Adult* is able to choose their response to any reaction that occurs, and their reaction to any response.

Instead of trying to control other people, learn to control your own personal experience and set clearer boundaries. People may attack you with accusatory language or try to initiate a reaction or conflict. Stay calm and take the time to respond responsibly, rather than react irrationally, especially if you find yourself responding with anger or counter attacks. The major difference between a response and a reaction is the time involved. Unlike the outburst of an immediate reaction, a response takes time to formulate a conscious choice for how to proceed.

The following six steps show how to negotiate stepping out of drama in relationships:

1. Identify which role(s) in the drama triangle are played by the person with whom you are engaged. Identify what role(s) are your tendency to step into when the other roles are played.

2. Consciously and respectfully make the choice to refuse to step into any unhealthy role being requested of you (victim, rescuer, or persecutor), and instead choose a healthier response or no response at all to their invitation to engage in the drama.

3. Observe their response, and if they become persistent, try explaining that you are not going to engage in the role they are requesting of you. If this fails, make a clearer statement by setting a clear boundary. This boundary includes stating the behavior they are exhibiting, why the behavior is unhealthy, and why you are choosing not to engage with them in this manner.

4. Respond to any anger or retaliation with non-reaction or clear statements explaining why there is no basis for their response to you.

5. Continually repeat steps one through four until there is movement out of the drama roles and into healthier behavior patterns. Allow time for the new paradigm of engagement to become clearly understood through several iterations and healthy repetitions.

6. Continually establish new healthy ways to engage while keeping yourself from being drawn into drama or having to respond to drama. Observe the other person's gradual change to a healthier paradigm or wish them well on departure from the relationship.

Throughout this process, each step will require observing the other's response to decide what your next step will be. When you change your behavior and step out of the drama role and dysfunction to a healthier role, you may find the person involved will retaliate by lashing out at you, getting angry, pouting, continuously complaining, withdrawing, or showing their anger in other ways such as suspending or terminating the relationship altogether. When you avoid reacting to these types of behavior with further

Victim, Persecutor, or Rescuing behavior, then you step out of the drama completely. Stepping out of the drama shows other people in your life there are consequences to their behaviors, and those consequences include removal of yourself from any drama or dysfunction.

Those entrenched or addicted to drama won't allow change to occur or won't change easily and will continue to try to get you on the hook for more drama or other unhealthy patterns of behavior. These behaviors are expected. People will use drama in the form of anger, protests, passive aggressive behavior, or more drama to divert attention away from the actual problem or transgression, or from their own bad behaviors. Thus, the focus becomes about their anger, denial, defensiveness, or attempts to engage you back in drama.

Sometimes confronting another's drama will be protested, and they will turn it around by accusing you of being the cause of the drama. This can be a form of passive aggressiveness, and these individuals are best called out for their resistance and avoidance each time it occurs. Most often the person will justify or deny their behavior. If they are unwilling to recognize their passive aggressiveness and make changes, then eventually distance may be the only recourse, because they will continually tend to justify their behavior as right without accepting personal responsibility for their behavior. The topic of passive aggressive behavior will be explored more in the next chapter.

Any retaliatory act confirms you are in an unhealthy relationship, unhealthy role, or engaged in drama. When you have changed the conditions of engagement, and the other person no longer gets whatever rewards they once obtained from the drama, they may retaliate in some manner to show their displeasure with the new way of relating. Getting any response of anger or withdrawal is a good indication that unhealthy roles were engaged. Be patient during this time so the person has time to shift with you to your new behavior, and to changes to the rules of engagement. Even though these changes are healthy in the long run, they will often be perceived at first as hurtful, alienating, and selfish, or they may feel you are punishing them or

162

pushing them away. Any negative reactions are expected because you have changed the rules of engagement and it is not yet clear how to re-engage in healthier behaviors. Your change to a healthier role in the relationship may cause the relationship to terminate. Sometimes ending the relationship or taking time to regroup is exactly what needs to happen, especially if the other person cannot stop playing the roles of the Drama Triangle. An example may be a Victim who lashes out because you no longer rescue them in response to every plea for help or "cry of wolf."

Other examples of stepping out of drama are a Persecutor who no longer gets satisfaction from punishing or hurting the Victim, because the Victim takes a stand and says "no more," or a Rescuer may become totally confused when a person they have been rescuing refuses their help and does exactly what is needed for themselves, by themselves.

Over time, you will come to recognize people who engage in drama and if they are capable of stepping in to healthier roles and healthier relationships, as *Adults* who no longer engage in drama or dysfunctional behavior. If this is not possible, then you can reevaluate your level of involvement with those people who cannot disengage from drama. Demeaning or controlling behaviors, unnecessary complaining, and other unhealthy behaviors always cause some form of separation. If you want healthier relationships, you have to choose to engage differently. It is insane to continually engage in the same patterns of dysfunctional behavior while at the same time expecting different outcomes. Stop wandering in your relationships, and start wondering *Why?*

You will also notice people in your life who want to stay in the drama because of some perceived payback, gratification, or control. They may justify playing their various roles with statements that attempt to justify their behavior. The Victim may say, "Poor me, look at all that is wrong in my life right now." The Rescuer may say, "But I am only doing this for you and trying to help you." And the Persecutor may say, "You deserve this anger or punishment from me because my needs were not met." These judgments and their variations are additional clear indications that unhealthy roles are being played. Seeing these signs and signals helps you to stay out of these roles with other people and within yourself.

It becomes a true relief and joy to step out of the Drama Triangle and out of dysfunctional behavior patterns and move toward engaging in healthy relationships. We may continue to step back into these unhealthy behavior patterns until we become aware our joy, happiness, and peace are more valuable to us than the resulting suffering we receive from unhealthy behavior or our involvement in unhealthy relationships.

Responsible *Adults* learn to ask for help when it is truly needed (Vulnerable) without engaging in persecuting behaviors. They learn to ask directly for what they need and want of others (Decisive) respecting the outcomes. They learn to provide help and advice to those who ask for help when help is truly needed (Empathetic) without needing to fix, rescue or solve other's problems for them without being asked.

Getting out of the drama roles will help you put your life in perspective. Eventually you will find there are much more enjoyable, interesting, and noble pursuits than the trivial games of drama. It may be difficult at first to meet people who are ready for healthy relationships. Be patient. They are out there. Some people may leave your life, some will take a break and others will resist or struggle to accept your changes. Be patient with yourself and with others during this time of adjustment to a new paradigm that will serve and sustain you and them. Reward heathier behaviors and consistency with acknowledgement and gratitude, rather than engaging in criticism or judgment of unhealthy behaviors.

CHAPTER TEN

Destructive Behavioral Statements

We all have extreme emotions, but each of us is individually responsible for modulating our emotions, words spoken, and any resulting behaviors so their expression is healthy and constructive in each interaction. Modulating our emotions requires that the outward expression of extreme volatile moods such as manic anger or the depths of depression must become consistently centered and balanced without the need for unhealthy expression of these extremes. A *behavioral statement* is any verbal statement, action, or behavior that can occur in our relationship interactions. Our goal as *Adults* is to exemplify *behavioral statements* that are positive, constructive, supportive, and respectful in our interactions with others by filtering our emotions and choosing constructive statements. Destructive *behavioral statements* include everything from rude, insulting, or degrading statements to violent statements and any *behavioral statement* in between which separates, or is unconstructive to maintaining healthy relationships. Destructive *behavioral statements* can be looked at based on their level of destructiveness and their overall impact to the relationship. When destructive *behavioral statements* do occur, there is a need to look at these individually and collectively in order to decide how to get the relationship back on track. When there is any doubt about the intent or severity of a person's behavior, then common decency and basic respect should be your guides. Negative or damaging *behavioral statements* fall into one of three basic categories, depending on their severity: cautionary behaviors, detrimental behaviors, and destructive behaviors.

Cautionary behaviors in some way betray trust in the relationship. Some of these might include:

Sharing personal or intimate details of your relationship(s) or someone else's relationship with another person

Telling untruths, partial truths or white lies that are hurtful

Labeling or name calling that is derogatory in nature

Failure to keep small commitments, such as not returning phone calls, emails, or agreed upon social meetings such as coffee or lunches

A non-reciprocal relationship in which one person is always giving or one person is always taking

Indecisive behavior causing continual waiting by one or both parties for a decision from the other

Isolated instances of passive aggressive behavior or unnecessary criticism

Detrimental behaviors may erode the relationship because of the repeated nature of these offenses. Some of these may include:

Being overly critical or humiliating in public or in front of friends or family

Regular failure to respond to communication or requests for communication

Failure to have open and honest communication

Repeated failure to keep commitments, either small or large

Inability to resolve small conflicts with a win/win for all involved

Inability to take responsibility for inappropriate behaviors or words spoken

Inability to apologize for inappropriate behaviors or words spoken

Using or manipulating a person for time or personal resources

Regularly recurring instances of passive aggressive behavior

No respect for boundaries set over time

Engaging in gossip or hearsay with no intention to help another

Unintentionally causing problems or drama in relationships

Occasional overuse or misuse of drugs or alcohol

Destructive behaviors are the most serious and unacceptable of the *behavioral statements*, whether they happen to you, in your presence, or to another person who is not present. Some of these behaviors include:

Physically abusive or violent behavior to you, another person, or an animal
Anger issues involving abusive language or violent behavior
Repeated passive aggressive behavior
Repeated failure to keep large and small commitments once boundaries have been set
Intentionally causing problems or drama in relationships repeatedly over time
Unwillingness or inability to resolve large conflicts
Extremely abusive or threatening language directed at you or another person
Demeaning, derogatory, or otherwise devaluing language that subordinates or subjugates you or another person either privately or publicly
Repeated dishonesty, lying, or not telling the whole truth
Engaging in breaking laws, or engagement of you to break laws
Repeated manipulative behavior for one's own gain or the gain of others when boundaries have been set
Failure to pay back agreed upon financial commitments, debts, or loans
Controlling words, actions, or behaviors that constrain who you are as an individual or constrain the relationship
Violent behaviors such as throwing objects or slamming doors
Unwanted attention or stalking behaviors
Regular overuse of prescription drugs, illegal drugs, or alcohol.
Emotionally abusive or manipulative behaviors

Sexually explicit, vulgar, or indecent behaviors in public places

Knowingly transmitting any illness or life threatening disease

The *behavioral statements* above are not conducive to healthy relationships, and depending on the severity are sufficient cause for a temporary pause, suspension, or reevaluation of the relationship. In some instances these behaviors are reasons for terminating a relationship, particularly when they are violent, physically abusive or emotionally abusive. A person who inflicts pain and suffering on anyone or inflicts pain and suffering on themselves should be considered to have limited capacity for healthy relationship dynamics. Suspending a relationship with a person exhibiting these extreme behaviors is the clearest boundary you can set until there is significant progress toward resolving their personal issues. These unacceptable behaviors indicate deeper problems that the person has not worked through, or what we often call "baggage," to a degree that he or she can interact with another person in a constructive, healthy, adult, or *Adult* manner. The healing of our inner child and integrating all of the traumas or stories of what our parents did, or didn't do for us, what happened or didn't happen to us, allows us to become whole and integrated healthy *Adults* who take personal responsibility for their life as it exists today, without blaming their present on their past.

Stress, tension, extreme emotions, and anger prevent us from seeing the truth and thinking clearly about our role in situations of drama or dysfunction. If you or anyone you know is regularly exhibiting one or more of these behaviors, there is a strong case for considering professional help or therapy to assist in the recovery of healthier behavior patterns.

It is not enough to have awareness or understanding of destructive behavioral statements, but rather to actually make changes or set boundaries that bring these unhealthy behaviors into healthier behaviors. A person who exhibits any of these behaviors in your presence requires the following actions on your part:

168

1. Tell the person exactly how his or her offensive words or behaviors have affected you or made you or others feel. Words can be just as violent as physical acts of violence.

2. Tell the person this behavior is not constructive to your relationship, and you feel uncomfortable with it. Depending on the severity, especially when violence or abusive language is involved, tell the individual to get professional help and then take a break from your relationship until they have made enough progress to engage in a healthy adult relationship.

3. Give the person a chance to apologize and explain what he or she was feeling and the reason for the behavior. In addition, the individual should make amends and rectify the objectionable behavior when possible.

4. Be open and allow the person the freedom to change and make positive moves to keep the relationship on healthy ground.

5. Be willing to forgive the individual for his or her behavior. We all make mistakes, but how we rectify our mistakes shows our true intention, love, and respect for each other and our relationships.

6. Ask the person to make a commitment to not repeat the destructive behavior ever again in your presence. If he or she does not agree, or is unwilling to agree, consider a temporary pause of the relationship until commitment can be made. In severe cases where the ego is responsible for justification of the negative behavior, terminating the relationship may be the best and healthiest option and the most loving decision for you and for the other person.

7. If a commitment was made to not repeat the abusive language or behavior, continue to monitor the commitment and hold the person accountable. Then, if a break in the commitment occurs, give fair warning, and then consider limiting your contact with this person or terminating the relationship.

Before going through the steps above, ask yourself the meaning of your relationship to this person in your life, and depending upon the severity of the behavior, whether you want the relationship to go forward or to end. Making this decision requires that you consider the frequency of this type of behavior and your willingness to invest your time, money, or energy going forward. Healthy relationships augment our lives by bringing joy, pleasure, and shared experiences; they do not diminish or take away who we are or what we enjoy.

Manipulating Behaviors

Manipulating behaviors are used to control another person, either knowingly or unknowingly. In this section, we will look at manipulating behaviors with examples of the most common types.

Using or manipulation occurs when the person being used believes that his or her best interests are being served by the intentions of the manipulator. In reality, the intentions are solely for the manipulator's benefit. Intention is the distinguishing factor to determine if a behavior is using or manipulative. Manipulating behaviors may be a ploy for some desired outcome of acquiring resources, such as money, time, sex, friendship, love, etc. Manipulation always involves a setup, but a person is usually unaware of the setup, trusting that the intention is for his or her benefit or for the good of the relationship. The opposite of using or manipulative behavior is to clearly and honestly state the desire or intention up front.

Using and manipulating behaviors are also the opposite of loving relationship behaviors. Love considers all of those involved, not just the needs of the person who manipulates to get their way. Using behavior can be subtle and hard to identify because the other person's intent is not clear initially, and often it is not seen or revealed except in hindsight. To avoid using or manipulating behavior is to ask, or be asked, for what is desired, and the reasons why it is wanted, all with full transparency.

Those who engage in using or manipulative behaviors can become

170

skilled opportunists, knowing how and when to use others to fulfill their own desires or needs. One way you can get a glimmer you are being used is by developing the awareness that interactions with a given person meet most of their needs, but your own reasonable needs are not getting met. Such opportunists may come into your life because doing so fulfills a need of theirs. Once that need is met, they go missing until you are needed again. Over time, you find there is no reciprocity of time and personal resources.

Another way to get clear is to ask questions, the answers to which clarify their intentions and the long-term goals of the relationship. If you listen and watch closely, you will see if in fact this individual is using you, and does not consider the relationship as long-term, but rather a relationship of convenience, useful when it meets their immediate needs. If the person is not being truthful or authentic with you in some way, you will sense it. There is often an element of ambiguity; things don't add up or make sense, or their behaviors do not match the commitment made. They may avoid making plans or commitments in advance and instead engage you when it is most convenient or accommodating for them or as their needs arise. If you stop giving your resources and there is a pull back or termination of the relationship, then this is usually a clear indication you were being used. Another form of manipulation is to make promises to do something and nothing happens to fulfill that promise. Revealing these behaviors will require time, but if a person is operating with the intent to use you, such a relationship is damaging and disrespectful of you and your resources.

Knowingly using a person is wrong and lacking in integrity. However, becoming aware of the signals that we are being used or manipulated occurs often only through hindsight. Once an awareness of being used exists, continued using behavior will eventually erode the relationship as you find yourself constantly setting and resetting boundaries to prevent the using behavior.

There are several manipulating behaviors common to relationships. One of these is making trouble. There are those people who persecute either consciously or unconsciously through stirring up trouble with others. These people like to needlessly "push buttons, yank chains, and stir pots." Stirring up trouble for the sake of trouble takes place because some people derive pleasure from the resulting chaos and use it as an opportunity to gain an advantage. For example, such people may position themselves to rescue others when the chaos unfolds. Persecutors of this type are best avoided at all costs.

Another common form of manipulation is the attempt to keep involved parties separate through exclusion. There may be an intentional exclusion of certain people that prevents normal interactions and allows the manipulator to orchestrate what each person hears, thinks, and believes as a means of preventing the truth of a situation to be revealed. Manipulators of this type often lie to one person in an attempt to hide their own faults or transgressions, and then separate people so the lie can continually be propagated. Be wary of anyone who keeps you separated from friends or family, because the intent may be manipulation through exclusion.

Unhealthy people may use the roles of Victim, Persecutor, and Rescuer to manipulate you into agreeing with their positions. They may feel insecure and need you to back them up, even when their behavior is dysfunctional or inappropriate. A Persecutor's behavior may not always be obvious or covert. More often the behavior can be passive aggressive and may involve non-verbal or passive acts that are hurtful or negative in nature. The Persecutor can appear nice and sympathetic on the surface, but underneath this façade can be anger, jealousy, manipulation, or malicious intent that gets expressed indirectly through passive aggressive behaviors. The aggression can be hard to pin down when not overt, but rather appears as a form of resistance such as avoidance, quiet stubbornness, not doing what was promised, being late or not showing up on time, etc. Dealing with passive aggressive people can be some of the most difficult relationships to navigate because such people consistently justify their behavior as right and avoid taking responsibility for hurtful actions, inactions, or the havoc they can cause.

Not only are passive aggressive people hard to deal with in personal relationships, but rarely can professional therapy help them: They become so skilled at justifying their passive aggressive behavior that they actually believe their stories of justification, thus leaving no way to break through to the truth.

A scapegoat is a person used to take the blame or responsibility for another's negative actions. Blame is never needed if everyone steps up and takes personal responsibility for their behavior. Scapegoating is usually persecuting behavior that directs responsibility for behavior to someone else. A Persecutor may use difficult life circumstances as an excuse to treat you or others badly. In these instances, the Persecutor usually flips back and forth between Persecutor and Victim by always having some difficult or horrible life circumstance by which they feel victimized. This puts you into rescue mode, and then when you do not rescue them, they may turn to the role of Persecutor.

Those who are caught in a Victim role may use their constant needs or cries for help to manipulate others for their time, attention, or other resources. The Victim's appetite for more may be insatiable: they want more money, more material items, more time, or more love, yet they are unwilling or unable to reciprocate any of these. Such hungry ghosts walk the earth looking for those willing and able to step in and fill all of their voids, exhibiting little or no regard for the needs of others.

A Rescuer may manipulate by withholding their personal resources like money, affection, love, and time until they receive what they want to receive in return. A Rescuer may use their resources as rewards to get what they want from others through obligation or indebtedness. Rather than engaging in generosity and healthy reciprocity, a Rescuer may maintain control by being the only one giving in the relationship. The Rescuer may be attempting to create his or her own rescue through rescuing others. A Rescuer may personalize the Victim's feelings and then try to step in and make things better for them so they too, can feel better.

173

Manipulating others or allowing others to manipulate us is not *Adult* behavior and does not help to cultivate personal or collective freedom. When we stop trying to rescue, change, control, fix, or manage other people, our lives become simpler and more joyful, both for us and for the people around us.

Dependent Behaviors

When we engage repeatedly in dysfunctional behaviors, it usually is the result of a pattern of dependency or co-dependency occurring in the relationship. Dependent behaviors can be healthy when the needs and expectations are natural, reciprocal, and cohesive in an interdependent relationship; however, they are unhealthy when engaged in the dysfunctional patterns of the Drama Triangle, and there are unfair expectations or unresolved conflicts involved.

Negative codependency occurs when one or both people are playing out roles on the Drama Triangle, or engage in dysfunctional behaviors, and continue to stay in the relationship enabling and/or manipulating each other in spite of these unhealthy behaviors. Becoming aware of *codependency* is the first step in avoiding roles that negatively enable these unhealthy behavior patterns to continue. Enabling occurs when we allow a person to continue a behavior hurtful to them, hurtful to us, or hurtful to others without stating a clear *No*, calling them out on their inappropriate words, actions, or behaviors, or not setting clear boundaries. Doing nothing can also be enabling, as can making excuses for another person's bad behavior. By being passive, not setting clear boundaries, or standing up for what is right, we can be just as destructive as the person doing the actual harm.

One example of enabling behavior is when you give money to an alcoholic who tells you they need it to pay their bills, and then they turn right around and use it to buy more alcohol. One of the most difficult aspects of enabling can be the enabler's belief they are actually helping another, when

174

in reality they are hurting the person by enabling them to continue their destructive behavior. If there is a clear end in sight, then you will want to provide help that will bring actual closure to an individual's problems. If the end is not clear, then whatever you do will probably continue to enable destructive behavior.

Negative enabling behavior can be much more subtle in our personal relationships, creeping in without our conscious awareness, and gradually becoming a problem that must be addressed. If one person is blamed and takes all the responsibility for the problems that arise all of the time, this is unbalanced, unhealthy, and another symptom of codependence. When you have been an enabler, setting a clear boundary usually causes some discomfort, turmoil, and in some cases may even end the relationship if the offending person is not willing to step back and see their unconstructive behavior in the relationship.

Finding your way out of unhealthy codependent relationships requires first identifying you are engaged in unhealthy codependent behaviors. Once you see this happening, staying in a codependent relationship is usually related to the fear that removing the dependent behaviors will cause the relationship to end or lead to physical or emotional abuse. The subsequent fear of being alone can also prevent productive change in unhealthy relationships. Fearful outcomes are perceived to outweigh the need to engage in a mutually healthier relationship that satisfies all involved. People stay in unhealthy codependent relationships because they are unaware of how to engage in healthy dependence, or they lack the knowledge of how to step out of dependent behavioral patterns.

Patterns of dependence or codependence are often learned from our families of birth and passed on from generation to generation. Until a person becomes aware of these dependent patterns of behavior, they will not be able to step outside them and develop healthier ways of relating. The next section looks at the steps we can take to remove ourselves from unhealthy dependent and codependent behaviors.

Making Healthier Relationship Choices

Once we learn to identify the signals of unhealthy involvement in relationships, we can start to make healthier choices regarding how we want to engage with others. We can choose to set better boundaries, to disengage entirely, or to not become engaged in these relationships in the first place. Any relationship lasting for any length of time has both good and the not so good experiences, but if the overall relationship is rewarding over time, room exists for all of it. A relationship laden with too many problems or issues to deal with properly at the beginning may tip the balance to more negative interactions making the relationship hard to sustain, perhaps even end it entirely.

People who have deep emotional hurts or unresolved emotional issues are often not ready to engage in a healthy relationship. If you observe people with extreme mood swings such as outbursts of anger or deep depression, encourage them to do the work they need to heal, including getting therapy if they want to work toward a healthy relationship. As previously stated, *everyone is personally responsible for modulating his or her own emotions and behaviors*. We are each responsible for our words and actions at all times without making excuses for them. Extremely emotionally charged words or behaviors are not conducive to healthy Adult interactions. A person who is verbally abusive may also have the potential for physical abuse. Physical, verbal, or psychological abuses are not acceptable behaviors in any relationship.

Women have been especially susceptible to emotional and physical abuse, which shows the need for men to advance in their ability to express or heal their underlying emotional issues. While emotional abuse can be subtle to an outsider, its effects can be just as devastating as physical abuse While the scars of physical abuse may heal in the short term, the scars of emotional abuse can be lasting and often take much longer to heal and overcome.

Getting out of abusive patterns often requires the help of a trained professional. The victim in an abusive relationship must also get help in seeing their unhealthy dependency on the abuser, as well as dealing with potential low self-esteem issues and the need for setting clear boundaries.

Betrayal can be a more subtle form of unhealthy behavior in relationships. Betrayal can include a romantic partner having an affair with someone outside of the relationship, being lied to, betrayal of confidential information, or deception in any form. When betrayal occurs, the person who betrayed the relationship owns responsibility for their behavior, related apologies, and in extreme cases for making amends for their betrayal if possible. Any betrayal is surmountable if both parties are willing to stay in the relationship and work through related issues as they arise. If there are repeated betrayals, this is potentially a reason to end a relationship, as a repeated pattern of betrayal indicates an unwillingness to change.

Getting involved in other people's relationship problems can be unhealthy for you, for others, and for the relationships involved. Tampering is the unhealthy involvement or interference in other's relationships. This form of tampering is often based on assumptions since the full story of others' problems is not known. What is known is often one-sided, often not fully understood, and ultimately not anyone else's business. A simple rule to follow for tampering is this: Don't get involved in other people's relationship problems or predicaments. Maintaining any relationship can be hard work, so don't give advice on others' relationships unless you are asked. If you are asked, it can be more effective and helpful to provide questions that help people to find the needed answers for themselves.

Some of these questions might be:

- How often does this behavior occur?
- How does the behavior he or she exhibits make you feel?
- What is the behavior you would like to see occur?
- What would life be like if this person were not in your life?
- Is this person getting help or willing to change?

It is important to not choose sides or insert yourself between two people who are having difficulties in a relationship. Also, it is wise to avoid involving other people in your own relationship problems without careful consideration. Getting involved in others' relationships often backfires and comes back to hurt potentially everyone involved. If you find yourself drawn in to others' problems, you can always state, "I am sorry you are having that experience. It would probably be best to talk with them about it directly." Or, for more serious problems "Have you considered seeking professional help?"

Too often people want to pull you into a conflict they are having with someone in order to garner support for their position, their view, or their behavior. Staying out of these situations, or at a minimum, remaining neutral and avoiding actively participating by taking sides keeps everyone clean in interactions that can become fraught with problems.

People will also sometimes try to engage in transitive relationships by attempting to connect with one person through another person. Transitive relationships are not possible, nor can they be fulfilling. Engage directly with another person, but avoid engaging in indirect relationships as these are usually forged with no true returns or desired outcomes.

A relationship of convenience is another form of unhealthy relating. Although some need is being fulfilled for one or both parties, the relationship of convenience does not adhere to all the elements of a healthy relationship. However, if all expectations are agreed upon up front, then these too can sometimes be sustaining.

People will often mistake needing someone as the basis for a relationship. We often need the emotional or financial support of others, but needs alone cannot be the only reason for being in a relationship. Needs comprise one element that unfolds over time, but other fundamentals of a good relationship must also be in place, such as enjoying a person's company, shared interests, shared values, and shared experiences. You cannot buy a person's company, affection, or love, and any relationship based on a financial arrangement is a business arrangement, not a relationship.

You might come across people who desire a relationship with you because you have wealth, a nice home, or some other resource desirable to them, but this cannot be the primary reason you are in relationship with them. In friendships, this is important to see early on. With regard to resources in romantic relationships, when all is considered, true love may be the greatest resource we can give or receive, and can offset shortcomings in financial ability or other resources.

Insecurity often causes problems in relationships if one or both people experience a sense of lack and then try to fill their lack with the other's love or resources. There may even be jealousy of the other's resources. Insecurity usually causes a constant state of judging and comparison of one's own condition to another's, which results in wasted energy. Insecurity can cause difficult behaviors such as over-protection or a desire to be in the other's company constantly because of distrust or a lack of intimacy.

Another manifestation of insecurity is competition. We all may meet people at times who would rather compete with us than be in relationship with us. Someone who is competing probably does not have your best interests in mind. The competition could be for success, a shared interest in someone else's time or affection, or for money, power, or even attention. Healthy personal relationships are not competitions. We want to have peers in our lives, not rivals.

Finally, time is one of our most valued resources. You will meet people who continually want your time and attention because it feeds their egoic need for time or attention. If someone requires an unhealthy amount of your attention, it usually indicates an underlying problem of egoic need or an inability to engage in real intimacy. Once you recognize this is what's at work, you can direct your attention toward developing more intimacy in the relationship if the person is capable.

Jealousy and Envy

Envy is a thought pattern stemming from the ego's need to have what it perceives as desired or missing. Envy often arises from coveting what another person is deemed to possess. Some of the most common objects of envy are money, power, achievement, material possessions, and relationships. Envy is another waste of our time, energy, and emotion, because it does not lead to any constructive behavior or bring joy to a relationship.

Jealousy is an emotion arising from insecurity in a relationship, when one person's connection to others is perceived as a threat to the relationship.

Jealousy and envy always alert us when we are not happy with some aspect of our lives or with ourselves. These emotions can signal our need to take action to get what we desire so feelings of jealousy or envy of others are removed.

To overcome feelings of jealousy or envy, we must first get clear about what we perceive is missing from our own lives. The object of jealousy may only be a pointer to what is truly desired. Ask yourself: *Do I really want _____, and if I had it would my desire be fulfilled?* Once you are clear on what you desire or feel is missing, then you must ask if this is what you truly want for yourself, whether it is really possible, and if you are willing to put forth the effort required to acquire what is desired.

We can become jealous, even when we are unclear what makes us jealous. Jealousy of something we do not want or do not want to spend the energy to acquire is wasted energy. If you truly desire something, the first step is to set clear goals and then a process for how you will achieve these goals. Going through this process to get clear on how true you are to your desire and your willingness to work for it often clears up any jealous feelings and helps us focus on what we might be willing and able to do for ourselves.

Jealousy in relationships can get us into trouble. Jealousy is not an emotion of good intention and can put others on guard. A tendency may arise to withhold or not share the object of jealousy. Jealousy of others can become overly childish and a warning sign of intense insecurity or lack of self-esteem. One's relationships with other people are no one else's business. Jealousy of other people's time together or another's happiness is also a waste of time and energy and clearly a failure to see where we are unhappy within ourselves or with our lives.

Jealousy in relationships can arise from a lack of trust or unfair expectations, especially if one person feels threatened by the relationships his or her partner has with others. If unfair expectations are in place, jealousy may be experienced when these expectations are perceived as being fulfilled by someone else.

If someone is jealous or envious of you for what you have, what you do, who you are with, or who you are as a person, these feelings can lead to destructive behaviors and be destructive to the relationship. For example, two men desire to date the same woman. Eventually the woman decides she is attracted to one of the men, and they develop a romantic relationship together. The other man becomes so jealous that he terminates his relationship with both the man and the woman who are engaged in the romantic relationship. In this situation, jealousy has led to inappropriate punishing behavior of the couple for their relationship and desire to engage romantically. Comparing your life to the lives of others is a waste of time; your goal is to have your own life experience. If you do not have the experiences you desire, strive to create them.

Jealousy can also be used to guilt trip others for something they have or their feelings for someone else. An overly jealous person can become manipulative in an attempt to control the times of interaction among friends, family members, or relatives. Jealousy usually indicates feelings of distrust, and trust must be re-established in the relationship and boundaries reset.

When your life is going well, people may become jealous of you. Accept that jealousy is a possible reaction to success, but resist the temptation to be jealous of others. Learning to replace feelings of jealousy and envy with indifference, or even more positively with happiness for others, will better serve everyone involved. When we wish others happiness and joy, this positive energy is often returned to us and attracts more of the same.

Judgmentalism

The ego tends to dislike, judge, or label what it does not understand or is not familiar with, and this causes separation, fear, and at its worst, war. Judging or labeling others is an unconstructive negative act that diminishes value, often for the purpose of inflating one's own sense of worth. Whenever we place value on something and then judge it as either bad or good, we are ultimately contributing to feelings of separation. Jesus' statement "Let he who is without sin cast the first stone."[10] illuminates our need to remove judgement of others, lest we be judged. Why would anyone feel they have the right to cast judgement on another? *We are all perfectly imperfect.* Our peace on this planet requires that we be vigilant in our awareness of the ego's need to judge and separate.

Judgment of another person or a group of people usually arises from ignorance. Comparing ourselves to other people is an unnecessary waste of time; we are all unique individuals with no criteria or standard of measure for the true complexity of who we are as human beings. Every person has intrinsic value and beyond this our ability for love, human kindness, integrity, and truth are considered measures of our awareness, not as a means to separate or judge. Discrimination is a form of judgmentalism that occurs when people are denied rights or given prejudicial treatment based on their race, age, sex, education, or sexual preference. Judging a person harshly or discriminating against them because of discriminatory or judgmental beliefs propagates a cycle of continued judgment and discrimination. The goal is to break through the ego's need to judge, label, or discriminate, and become free

---

[10] The Holy Bible, King James Version, John 8:7

to experience everything directly as it exists, not as how you believe or assume it exists.

What do we do when we encounter judgmentalism from others? When you are in the presence of someone who makes judgmental statements, your best response may be to have no response at all, showing them that you will not agree to or support judgmental statements. Sitting quietly without responding does not judge the person and gives no further energy to their judgment. Reacting to or correcting judgmental behavior can make the situation worse and potentially brings you into judgment of the person who is being judgmental. If the judgmentalism was extreme and made in the company of others, then addressing your concern with them alone may better serve to help them understand their judgmental statement.

To judge another is ultimately to be in judgment of oneself. We cannot judge another unless we have awareness within ourselves of the same flaw, fault, shortcoming, fear, or insecurity we are capable of projecting onto others as judgments. You will often see judgments cast by those who are actually perpetrators of the very behavior or characteristic they judge in others. Protesting too much in this manner may be an indicator of personal guilt or projection of the same characteristic being judged.

Judgments of others are by their nature biased, because they are based only on our personal knowledge, thoughts, or perceived standards, which may themselves be flawed or inaccurate. By whose standards, measures, and requirements is anyone to be judged? The more judgmental you are, the more separation you will actually experience and find in the world, because judgment of others causes separation from others and ultimately contributes to bondage rather than to freedom. Understanding judgmentalism brings you to care less about what other people think of you, and to stay grounded in your truth while stepping out of the limiting or judgmental beliefs of others.

No one has the right to judge another person based on gender, lineage, status, health, color, age, weight, body type, sexual preference, disease, or illness. None of these individual attributes completely define a person, but

183

are merely subdivisions of the true value, diversity, and uniqueness of each human being. Your status in life or in society does not define who you are or make you better than anyone else. Measures of status do nothing but separate us. Equality brings us together under the unifying condition of life having the human experience.

Maturity means seeing another person as a whole human being with a respect for the diversity of all people. Letting go of judgmentalism is a sign of becoming a responsible and compassionate *Adult* with a basic respect for all beings. We all have equal intrinsic value because we were born into this human form and into this world to share this time together. Our shared humanity matters more than our perceived differences. Expression of our diversity leads to our greatest achievements and ultimately allows the human species to evolve.

Never diminish what you do not understand. This is the biggest mistake of the human ego. Our differences and our uniqueness are causes for celebration and appreciation, not for judgment or discrimination. The diversity of cultures and the people of those cultures add interest and depth to the human experience. Embracing diversity brings us closer to understanding life in all its various forms.

When any group or person is required to conform to one ideal or is discriminated against, we should all fear for our human rights, for the seeds of persecution begin with a judgmental thought or a discriminatory act that leads to separation rather than inclusion. All of the negative behaviors of separation (hate, greed, jealousy, labeling, judging, denial, repression, grasping) arise from a lack of awareness of the divine unity of all beings. Hate occurs only when the ego forgets its connection to everything and everyone. The philosophy of equal rights means more than mere tolerance. Tolerance alone is not equality. Hatred and bigotry practiced under the presumption of religious beliefs does not define a true spiritual path but merely a system of false beliefs.

Stereotyping is another type of judgmentalism in which assumptions are made that one attribute of a group is applicable to all people of that group.

Prejudice is a form of judgmentalism in which we have preconceived negative opinions or beliefs having no basis in truth, reason, or knowledge. The ego protects its need to be right while it rejects or judges what it doesn't understand as wrong. So, the first thing to notice is judgments are beliefs, values, or comparisons you or someone else has literally *made up*.

Comparison can be used by the ego to differentiate and separate, often so it can feel better about itself. We often judge a person as bad or wrong, when what we may be experiencing is a dislike of a particular behavior. Learning to clearly distinguish behaviors we do not agree with or dislike allows us to then set boundaries for the offensive behavior, to provide direct feedback, or to ask for the behavior we would prefer. This approach takes us out of the judgment process and into an interaction where more understanding of individual behaviors might be reached.

Self-judgment is also one of our most limiting belief systems because it keeps us enslaved to patterns of behavior not conducive to being fully self-actualized. Our harshest criticism can come from the self-critic within and limits our ability to explore and discover all we can be. If you feel overly judgmental or critical of yourself, take it as an indication you may need to make a change. Self-judgment is self-limiting behavior if we do not take the necessary steps to change what we deem limited or unworthy within ourselves.

When the standards by which we judge ourselves are unfair and unachievable, learning to discern what is true and what is false leads us to create fair expectations of ourselves.

If we are overly critical of ourselves, then we will have a tendency to be overly critical toward others. Learning to recognize the critic within allows us to see how we may also be overly critical of others.

Judgmentalism can become pervasive to our thoughts once allowed to enter, and when left unchecked we become gradually more judgmental of everybody or everything. Time and vigilance are needed to eliminate judgmentalism from the thought processes. Changing our judgments begins with awareness of each time we engage in judging. Once we recognize our patterns of judgmental thoughts, we shift these thoughts into life-affirming positive statements rather than contributions to increased negativity.

The next step is to learn to respond with engaged neutrality to the world around you. If you find yourself judging something negatively, allow your mind to see other options and explore the positive aspects. If you find yourself getting overly positive with feelings that are contrived or untrue, allow yourself to also see the neutral or non-positive attributes to reestablish balance. Regularly exercising these varying positions will eventually bring you to a place of neutrality and gradually remove the need to judge anything. Eventually, it becomes clear in each moment we can choose which thoughts serve us best. We reach an awareness of judgmentalism for what it is, a habitual mental pattern we can choose to engage or disengage, eventually disarming this pattern's hold on us. This might take some effort at first, but eventually you won't waste your time in negative and unconstructive thought patterns. You will begin to appreciate all people just as they are and life just as it is. This allows others freedom to be who they are. You come to understand judgmentalism actually takes energy to sustain, while acceptance takes no energy. Why waste time and energy in an activity that does nothing to enrich you, others, or your relationships with others?

There is a difference between being judgmental and having personal desires or intentions. You do not have to condone or enable poor behavior, but also you do not have to judge others for their behavior. If any behavior on the part of another person is inappropriate or simply not your preference, then simply let them be who they are and go your own way. You have the right to have your own desires, preferences, and intent. Getting to know who you are and your own personal desires and goals gives direction to your life. At the same time you can allow others freedom to be who they are, just as you would like this same freedom given to you.

There is a form of judgmentalism commonly cloaked as assumption. Assumptions are made when there are preconceived ideas about what happened, what will happen, what another person is thinking, or what the reason is for a person's behavior, rather than getting the facts of what has transpired. An assumption is a thought or conclusion for which there may be no proof. Instead of believing the mind's tendency to think it has it all figured out when it comes to how another person thinks or behaves, always question the beliefs in your own mind first and ask for the facts. If you do not understand someone's behavior, ask why he or she behaved in a certain way, especially when the behavior is harmful to you, to your relationship, or to someone else. Avoiding assumptions is particularly important in long-term relationships or marriages. While you may think you know how a person will respond to you, give them the freedom to change and respond in new ways, because we all continually change and grow, which means our responses change also. Because assumptions are often without a foundation of truth, these put everyone involved on shaky and uncertain ground. If you assume anything, assume you may not have enough information to make any assumptions. More often than not, assumptions lead to more chaos and ambiguity in our interactions, rather than clarity and peace.

Discernment differs from judgmentalism. One can discern the quality of something based on preferences without being judgmental, by making a comparison to a known standard of quality, a desired quality, or non-judgmental personal preferences. Discernment by comparison brings us clarity on the value of fine workmanship or human achievement, but requires there be publicly agreed upon standards, knowledge, or qualities to measure against. Do not confuse judgmentalism with the ability to discern quality or to express one's personal preferences that do not judge or discriminate.

Labeling is another form of judgmentalism, yet more subtle. The ego loves to attach labels to name everything and identify differences through these assigned labels. Labels, particularly negative labels, limit us to the definition of the ascribed label and can be used to subjugate and divide us.

187

We cannot allow ourselves to be defined by the labels or judgments that are projected on to us by others. Once a label is ascribed, is it for the moment or for forever? How does a label ever get removed once assigned? Should a positive label entitle us in some way or mean we have more value? Labeling everything as good or bad, right or wrong is a dualistic approach to life. Since everything just *is*, there is no need to ascribe a label to it. What we perceive as bad or difficult may be some of our greatest gifts of learning and awareness. What we perceive as good for us may keep us in bondage and servitude for the remainder of our lives. What we perceive as bad may be exactly the lesson or knowledge we need to evolve. We really never know what is truly good or bad for us, except when we look back in hindsight to see the lessons we've learned.

Is it possible to accept where you are in your life now without labeling yourself, others and everything else? Is it possible to accept the circumstance of your life without judgment? It is possible through acceptance. Through acceptance, you can find your way to ever-new levels of peace and awareness.

In summary, tolerance, inclusion, neutrality, and equanimity are the opposites of judgmentalism, condemnation, blame, labeling, and assumption. Judgments never come close to defining the complexity and beauty of any human being based on the ideas of one person, one group, or even the collective beliefs of a society. What eventual purpose does our judgment serve us for evolving? Nothing is gained, nothing is lost, and nothing is achieved. We waste our time and energy when we engage the mind in judgmentalism. When we make it a practice to become less judgmental, knowing we are all equal, then equanimity will arise as a viable solution for all of humanity going forward.

Gossip

What is gossip and is it ever appropriate? When it comes to the care and maintenance of all our relationships, including our communities at large, gossip is generally a negative energy saying more about the nature of the person gossiping than anyone they may be gossiping about.

Gossip generally occurs when talking about another person while they are not present, often about their adversities, their behaviors, or their personal relationships, which neither serves to help them nor you to deal with them. Gossip can be any information with no intention of helping another, to help solve their problems or is untrue. Maintaining healthy relationships with others requires we do not engage in gossip about them! You are responsible for your business and not the business of others. Live your life and tell only your story; more importantly let other people live their life and tell their own story.

You will meet people whose entire conversation centers on hearsay or talking about others. You can always tell the difference between gossip and constructive or intimate conversation by looking at the intent of the person who is gossiping. If the person's intent is simply to share the news or adversities of another person, and there is no intent to help the person being discussed, then this is simply gossip, a waste of time, and potentially hurtful to others. Gossip can also lead to hearsay. Never act on hearsay without verifying facts first. A lot of damage is done to relationships when hearsay becomes the basis for actions taken.

It's possible to observe the life circumstances of others, and utilize it for one's own knowledge, insight, and intuition, rather than gossip. A good rule to follow in these situations is *if you don't have anything nice to say, then don't say anything at all*. Another rule to follow is *if you are not willing to say something to someone's face, then don't say it behind his/her back or to*

189

others. The exchange of ideas makes for good conversation, while mere gossip about others is boring and potentially harmful.

People who gossip usually want to gather information about others so they can share or relay this information through further gossiping. In its worst form, gossip can lead to collusion where private or personal information is revealed to be hurtful in nature to one or more people. You also encounter people who use gossip as a way of entrapping others to say something negative about another person, which they then turn around and use as leverage by relaying what has been said. Their intent is usually to gain favor or respect. With an *Adult* who is aware of what is occurring, it has the opposite effect of diminishing one's trust and respect for the gossiping person. No support given for this type of interaction or the gossip provided is the best course of action.

Usually the person gossiping somehow feels important, yet the gossiper has no real power, rather it is more about personal lack of self-esteem and preying on the hardship of others. For these reasons and many more, stay out of gossip all together.

Gossip is not intimate conversation, and while some relationships may be forged on this shaky ground, both parties know they could become the topic of gossip at any point by the person they gossip to. It becomes obvious if a person is willing to gossip about others, then they are probably likely to gossip about you. Trust does not evolve in relationships with a high degree of gossip as their basis, because the involved parties know what they say or do may become gossip for another person.

It is acceptable to talk about another person when the conversation centers on someone you both know, and you are discussing aspects of a person's behavior particular to you both, or you are looking for some advice or input on how to deal with a person, their behavior, or the relationship you have with them. It could also center on how to help a person who is going through a difficult life situation, or how to navigate difficult behavior if both parties have firsthand knowledge or experience with the behavior being

190

discussed. If someone asks you direct questions about another person with no other intent other than to "get the gossip", then a direct response to "Go ask this person directly" is the only correct response. This sets a clear boundary and lets them know you are not willing to engage in discussing private information about another person. It also allows them to discern what is actually appropriate to disclose or to discuss.

Gossiping about other people is immature, unconstructive, and a waste of energy. Taking the time to discuss the suffering of another person is not the activity of an *Adult*, and be clear to anyone that tries to have this type of conversation you are not interested in hearing the personal details of anyone who is not present, unless that person decides to share those details. This is an important boundary to set with yourself and with others. Having the consideration to confirm any rumors or gossip pertinent to close friends is a must before passing judgment or making assumptions.

Gossip can sometimes be an avoidance of intimacy, for those who lack the skills for meaningful or intimate conversation will engage in gossip instead. These people talk about others because it takes the responsibility of vulnerability off of them while shifting the focus to the vulnerabilities of others. You will recognize this in people who struggle with intimacy and are trying to find other ways to engage. If someone comes to you with gossip, then beware; there is every probability they are most likely sharing your personal information with other people as well. Gossip that does nothing to support the connection and community we all share is ultimately destructive in nature and best refrained from.

CHAPTER ELEVEN

Understanding Conflicts in Relationships

Conflicts occur to all of us at some point in our lives. Conflicts in personal relationships can occur through how we set boundaries and share our resources. Similarly, on a larger scale, countries have often gone to war over boundaries and protection of resources. Historically, the emphasis has been resolving conflicts with war rather than finding solutions that work for all. Developing conflict resolution skills is essential to how we go forward in peace on this planet.

It is our personal responsibility as responsible *Adults* to negotiate conflicts fairly and to a peaceful resolution. People often avoid conflicts or end relationships because they do not have the skills necessary to negotiate conflicts. Our ability to live together on this planet going forward depends on our ability to learn to resolve conflicts in a constructive manner for everyone involved. In this chapter, the skills of conflict resolution are examined from several perspectives so we can see how important these skills are in living peacefully with others and how to incorporate these skills into our lives.

First you discern if an actual conflict has occurred or if what is happening is simply a difference of opinion or a matter of personal preference. Differences of opinion and personal preferences are best resolved through amicable negotiation. Beyond these forms of disagreement, this chapter addresses the skills needed to resolve conflicts.

Conflicts can occur for many reasons, but these usually center on disagreements about beliefs, opinions, resources, boundaries, or miscommunication. A conflict can also be a simple failed expectation, but usually they arise from an egoic need to defend some resource, opinion, position, or belief. Conflicts also occur because of incongruent behavior or behavior lacking in integrity. Example: people not doing what they said they would do or failing to meet their commitments, which causes additional conflict.

There is a big difference between just expressing beliefs or opinions in a constructive argument and having a conflict over beliefs and expectations. The end result of an argument or debate can be constructive, allowing each person a better understanding of the other, their beliefs or opinions, or the situation being discussed. Both people must grant permission for this type of constructive argument, and agreement to the possible outcome that they may ultimately disagree. Arguments can become more extreme or develop into conflicts when arguments escalate into extreme disagreements where acceptance of eventual disagreement is refused. These conflicts are where clear skills of understanding conflicts and the means for conflict resolution are essential.

Whenever you find yourself defending any position, belief, or resource, the ego is clearly engaged. The ego's propensity to defend its position is the origin of conflicts. Everyone is entitled to their beliefs and has the right to their resources, whether we agree with them or not. No one is entitled to impose their beliefs on others, nor take the resources of others unfairly or without their permission.

When a conflict occurs, there can be only three outcomes: 1) the conflict is discussed and resolved; 2) the conflict remains unresolved or 3) both people can agree to disagree based on their beliefs in their positions, which can be a form of resolution. A conflict is resolved when both parties are in agreement on a particular issue, or both parties agree to go forward with disagreement. Agreeing to disagree can work in situations where the conflict does not involve unhealthy or destructive behavior.

Conflicts can be obvious and direct, or much more passive and indirect. While both must be addressed in relationships, the more passive and indirect conflicts can be much subtler and thus easier to overlook. A subtle conflict can arise from a difference of opinion or failed or unfulfilled expectations. Over time, the repetition of subtle conflicts can build until they too can have

193

lasting effects on the relationship. You have to work continuously at resolving issues as they arise. It is worth a bit of pain in the moment, to avoid a huge collapse later.

Most conflicts in relationships can be resolved by simply giving up the ego's need to be right. One of the most human things you can do is be vulnerable and admit your mistakes. Following this, an apology with the two simple words, "I'm sorry," heals multitudes of hurts and lifts the relationship to a new level of trust and respect. The most typical conflicts occur when one person is not willing to admit their part in the issue, or they feel strong about their position and are not willing to apologize so true healing can occur. In the face of any conflict with another person, choosing your response is all you have control over. When each person is able to take responsibility for his or her part, the relationship is moved forward into deeper trust and intimacy. A conflict dynamic always takes at least two and on some level both are always responsible for its continuation or for its resolution.

Very often when a conflict arises, you will find a person whose ego wants to exert control over another. This usually unfolds over time, where one person always feels they are right in their position and the other person always wrong, which leaves them feeling alone, unheard, and not getting their needs addressed in the relationship. Conflicts should not be used to subjugate or divide people, but ultimately to bring them closer together. For this to occur, the views, feelings, or concerns of everyone involved must be heard and acknowledged.

One of the benefits of resolving a conflict is the huge feeling of relief following which allows us to move forward unburdened and with healthier relationships. If one or both people do not value the relationship enough to get back to a place of comfort and ease, the relationship is on uncertain ground and may be heading for failure. Avoiding or running from conflicts will eventually inhibit one's ability to interact effectively with other people. Learning to confront conflicts directly and constructively will serve all of your personal and business relationships well throughout your life.

Conflict Resolution

The key to healthy maintenance of relationships is how each person approaches resolving conflicts. No matter how good the relationship, at some point people disagree about something, and a conflict, either small or large, will arise. Leaving a conflict in an unresolved state can have lasting effects on the relationship. Unresolved conflicts are usually remembered and often build with time to have much bigger implications. Resolving conflicts keeps us out of the unhealthy areas of building resentment and distrust. Conflict resolution allows ongoing care and trust to build a solid foundation that sustains relationships. Our shared ability to resolve conflicts leads to healthier relationships.

No one person can ever fulfill our every desire, either in a friendship, family or romantic relationship. Expectations often creep into our most intimate relationships, but relationships are always healthier when unfair or unreasonable expectations are avoided. The people with whom we choose relationships during our lifetime provide an array of different needs at different times. Our expectations are always shifting and changing as we go through the different stages of life. Often conflicts arise because unfair expectations or demands are being placed on one or both parties in a relationship.

Conflict resolution can lead to collaboration on a solution to a problem. Both parties must first be willing to realize the reason for the conflict is often simply not getting one's needs or expectations met. Reaching this moment of realization that an expectation is not being met begins the process of conflict resolution. With this observation, we can then ask ourselves the following series of questions:

➢ Is the expectation fair?
➢ Can the expectation be fulfilled?
➢ Are you willing to work toward a resolution?

➤ Is the other person willing to work toward a resolution?

All of these questions help us set the stage for a healthy encounter with a clear intent to resolve conflicts. If both people do not share this intent then the conflict may take time to resolve, not resolve at all, or cause the relationship to end. There is a quote from *A Course in Miracles* that asks: *Would you rather be right or would you rather be happy?* An *Adult* in relationship with others knows all of our expectations cannot be met all of the time, and when resolving conflicts, the spirit of compromise always prevails.

When people engage in relationships from the Healthy Triangle (Chapter Nine), without a Victim, Persecutor, or Rescuer at play, there will be a sincere attempt to resolve a conflict in an *Adult* manner.

Respect plays a valuable role in conflict resolution: You may not agree with a person's beliefs or opinions, but you can still respect that individual and their position. Becoming your own fair witness in a conflict means you are open to see both sides of the conflict while maintaining a desire to understand the truth of both positions. This allows you to fairly assess both sides and to apologize or adjust your position accordingly if needed. Conflict resolution is not about getting even with another person or about winning or only having the conflict resolve your way. Resolution may require a compromise of both positions held, rather than any one position or view being accepted. Both people must value the relationship enough to make the effort to get back to a place of peace and resolution by respecting each other's needs and positions. Without this willingness, conflicts are more difficult to resolve and affect the relationship long term.

When unfair expectations or conflicts do arise, space in which the conflict can be resolved is needed. Create space and time so communication and trust can be reestablished. It helps to remain open, rather than overreacting or punishing the messenger when what is presented does not meet your expectations or desires. Create space on neutral ground if possible, and interact face to face. If neither of these options is possible,

196

communication should take place through any means that allow both participants to be heard through safe and neutral interactions.

To begin the process of conflict resolution, assure the other person by telling them what the relationship means to you and express your desire to resolve the conflict as soon as possible. If either person feels intense anger or hurt about a given situation, it may be necessary to stop and wait until most if not all of the emotional charge has dissipated. When there are extreme emotions, you can tell the other person you want to resolve the problem, but you prefer to wait until you both can talk without extreme emotional reactions, particularly when anger is involved. When thoughts or ideas are delivered with anger, the meaning is lost or diluted. We tend to respond to anger with anger, rather than hearing the meaning of what is being said. If emotionally charged feelings need to be expressed, expressing them with words only and without the associated emotional charge gives them a better chance of being received and heard.

Before attempting conflict resolution, the following considerations are helpful to prepare:

➢ Get clear on your feelings and be able to express them directly and honestly with regard to the specific words, actions, or behaviors causing the conflict for you.
➢ Get clear on what your needs and expectations are, and then be open and willing to adjust them, modify them, or even let them go.
➢ Be fair and reasonable about your needs or expectations and ask yourself if the person can fulfill your needs or expectations. Is it reasonable to ask him or her to do so?
➢ Be clear about what a fair and reasonable outcome would be for both of you.
➢ For behavioral conflicts, explain how the words or behaviors affected you and made you feel rather than attributing labels of bad or good to the conflict.

Once engaged in attempting to resolve a conflict:

➤ Get clear on what exactly the current conflict is about, and keep your focus on your intent to resolve it.

➤ Come into the discussion with an honest intention of finding a resolution.

➤ Remove your ego's need to be right.

➤ Know your part in the conflict, and be willing to take personal responsibility for inappropriate behavior or misperceptions leading to the conflict.

➤ Deal with any related emotional issues one by one until they are resolved, and then continue to work toward a constructive conflict resolution.

➤ Don't bring up unrelated issues, problems, or past situations that distract from the current conflict, but rather focus on the facts of the current conflict first.

➤ If the conflict centers on a repeated behavior over time, then use the current instance to address the repeated behavior.

➤ Keep the communication open, honest, and continuous. Agree to hear each other's thoughts and feelings without interruption until all are understood, diminish, and a resolution is found to the satisfaction of both.

The Six Keys to Conflict Resolution

Following are the six essential keys to conflict resolution, listed in order of usual occurrence. The sequence can vary, and some steps may need revisiting more than once for final resolution to occur.

1. Show Up: The first step to resolution is for both people to show up in person to admit and agree that a conflict has occurred. If either person denies a conflict has occurred, or avoids resolution, then no resolution can begin. When conflicts are resolved in person, a richer long-term solution and experience is provided. If face-to-face is too difficult or not possible, then a phone conversation can begin the process. When you show up with an intention to resolve the conflict, you show a person you care enough about them and the relationship to resolve the conflict.

2. Be Willing: Both people must care enough to willingly resolve the conflict. If either party is not willing to recognize a conflict has occurred, or not willing to engage to resolve the conflict, then resolution does not begin nor is it possible.

3. Take Responsibility: The next step in conflict resolution is to take full responsibility for any harmful or hurtful behaviors, actions, or words with a clear statement of each of these and an apology for each. You will gain more respect and admiration when you are willing to step up and take full responsibility for your part in the conflict without needing a prompt. This responsibility cannot be one-sided, as both parties in any conflict usually have something for which they need to take responsibility. You can only be responsible for your part, and then be open and welcome the other to step up and take responsibility for their part. Someone must always take the first step, however if there is no movement on the other person's part toward this important first step, then asking them to take responsibility may begin the discussion. How each party handles taking responsibility for their actions during any conflict often determines how the conflict will resolve, and how the relationship will go forward.

If each side does not take personal ownership for their part in the conflict, one person may feel they were vulnerable and responsible while the other person was not. This situation can lead to more feelings of imbalance in the relationship, and take away from the trust and respect for each person involved in the relationship. When both parties are able to take personal responsibility for their parts in a conflict, the conflict moves more quickly toward resolution.

4. Listen: Communication during times of conflict is important for resolution. Take the time to listen and hear what the other person is saying and understand their position before you react, respond, or get defensive. Listening to each side's concerns and feelings without interruption and with empathy and openness to the other's point of view is key. If you think a person is not hearing what you are saying or what you are asking for, then ask them directly to acknowledge what you have said. If you believe your position is right, then defend it firmly but politely with an openness to hear the other person's position and justification. Being right is often open to personal interpretations of the meaning of "right" in a given situation. Remaining flexible in order to see other views or perspectives aids in the communication process.

Both parties must be fair, reasonable, and honest in their discussion of the conflict. Be flexible in your position if possible without taking away from who you are as a person, or what you believe.

5. Clarify the Conflict: Make clear decisions on areas or concerns on which you disagree and on those with which you both agree. Then continue to discuss each side's perspective until understanding, agreement, or resolution is reached.

In some conflicts, clarifying each other's positions or motivations may be the only resolution attained or the only resolution needed. The resolution to a conflict should not be the creation of another conflict. Sometimes this is unavoidable, especially if there are similar unresolved or recurring conflicts from the past. It may be important to agree that more time is needed to resolve each conflict, and then come back together when all conflicts can be clearly identified, articulated, and resolved. Keep a given conflict in perspective. When conflict does occur, it is important not to make a smaller conflict larger than it actually is, or similarly to trivialize a large conflict.

If, during the negotiation of the conflict, your position changes or is found to be false, then stand down and concede. Having to be right, becoming steadfast or stubborn, is what makes a conflict a lasting battle. So few are willing to make concessions, which often resolve most, if not all, conflicts. An open and continuous flow of communication is important if a conflict goes unresolved for an extended period of time. For longer periods of resolution, keep your behavior consistent in your interactions as much as possible. Changes in behavior such as pulling away or stopping regular communication will be perceived as terminating behaviors and show an unwillingness to move forward toward resolution. Remaining responsive keeps the communication ongoing. If one party needs to communicate or is expecting an answer to a prior communication, and the other party does not respond, this can be seen as passive aggressive behavior to control the interaction and is not constructive in the resolution process. If you ask for a response or the other person asks for a response when navigating a difficult situation, a response is better given, rather than avoided.

6. Find Agreement: The final steps in conflict resolution are to make any needed agreements on how to resolve the areas of conflict with apologies or actionable steps, in the hope of avoiding the same type of conflict in the future. If it feels right, discuss at some point how you might make course corrections next time to avoid the type of conflict. You might create commitments that both parties agree to abide by to prevent the same conflict from arising again. If a particular conflict continually occurs, then the first step is for both parties to agree on a commitment of how to handle it in the future. If the commitment on how to handle a recurring conflict is broken and the conflict continues to arise, depending on the severity, it may be cause for changing the form of the relationship, such as moving from dating to a friendship, or from a friend to a casual acquaintance. Repeated failures to keep commitments made during conflict resolution cause further damage to the relationship.

Agreement, apologies, forgiveness, and understanding are the possible outcomes and at least one of these is eventually reached for peaceful resolution. Two or more of these brings lasting effects, as well as the potential for deeper understanding and intimacy. Being overly apologetic or overly gracious cannot be used as a means of concession to resolve a conflict. However, it is always easier to resolve conflict, than to maintain the distance a conflict creates over time.

When extreme conflicts do arise, get clear that *it is often a behavior you don't like rather than the person you don't like*. This helps to approach the conflict by focusing on the offending behavior, and not by passing judgment

201

on the person involved. When there is damage done during a conflict, the relationship can be restored through apologies, forgiveness, and any additional reparative or healing actions.

It takes bravery and courage to stay involved in conflict resolution rather than to walk away. Both sides must want a resolution that is agreeable and suitable to the needs of both involved, or someone will leave the interaction feeling as though there are doubts, conditions, or unresolved issues arising from the conflict.

Some people will want to hold you accountable for your hurtful words or bad behavior even after you have admitted your fault and apologized. This behavior is another means of control and does not lead to resolution of the conflict. If you were big enough and vulnerable enough to put yourself out there to admit your wrongdoing or recant what was said, then the optimum response occurs if the other person reciprocates and is big enough to forgive you and let it go completely.

Even though a conflict can end with two people agreeing to disagree, there can be a respectful conclusion at which point both people feel strongly about their position and do not want to concede. If a person continually agrees to disagree just as a matter of principle or from an egoic need to win or not concede, this is probably a reason for concern as it may be a sign of potential problems in the relationship.

With practice, the process of conflict resolution becomes easier. The steps may vary, but when two people step up and take personal responsibility for their parts in the conflict, a deeper trust and mutual respect can unfold, and there is a real chance for lasting resolution leading to deeper intimacy from the conflict resolution process.

What to Avoid in Conflicts

Conflict resolution is not only about having the skills to resolve a conflict, but also about having awareness of what hazards might diminish or derail the resolution process. As much as you can, keep the conflict between you and the other person without getting others involved. Bringing outsiders into conflicts often brings both opponents and advocates: Everyone will have an opinion. If you have a trusted friend or fair witness who can provide balanced feedback, you may want to engage that individual. Otherwise, much of the time, involving others unnecessarily can complicate the conflict resolution process.

Avoidance of resolving a conflict can also be damaging as time goes on. A lack of response can indicate passive aggressive behavior, if avoidance is intentionally used to avoid communication or to punish another. Getting a conflict resolved as quickly as possible, rather than letting it drag on, serves everyone involved directly and indirectly. As more time goes by, the less likely the original conflict will be resolved, and this can deepen the initial hurt that occurred or build more misunderstanding of the original conflict. A series of unresolved conflicts gradually builds resentment, especially if they favor one person in the relationship or are hurtful to either. Unresolved, these can eventually lead to anger or passive aggressive behavior.

In more intimate loving relationships, the words "I love you" are sometimes used as a way to pacify and avoid the challenge of conflict resolution or the issues that created the friction in the first place. Loving someone means you are willing to take responsibility for your part in a conflict, which includes putting real actions, behaviors and meaning to the words "I love you."

It is also important not to use a conflict as a means of punishing another who has done wrong, especially if the person is willing to take personal responsibility for their part in the conflict, make amends for their actions, and show an intent to resolve the conflict. Punishing someone for their actions assumes a Persecutor role, and creates a new conflict for resolution, and is not conducive to resolving the original conflict.

An angry or agitated voice or tense body language elicits the same response. Talk as calmly as possible when trying to resolve conflicts as a calm voice elicits a calm response. Should the act of trying to resolve a conflict create more angst or tension, step away from resolution until both of you can approach the situation without emotional charge. Violence is never the way to resolve a conflict, even if violence is the source of the conflict. Demonstrations of violence never truly resolve conflicts, and violence is never acceptable. This is why laws and judicial systems were created and put into place. No one is above the agreed upon laws, including those in place to enforce these laws.

Avoid condescending words or behaviors that imply superiority, as they make a person feel as if you are beyond reproach, "right" or speaking down to them. None of us like being talked down to, or condescension, and this type of interaction is not only unconstructive, but also has the potential to trigger additional issues needing resolution.

Blame is best avoided during conflicts, as blame usually causes more feelings of resentment. When all involved in a conflict take full responsibility for their part in the conflict, blame is not needed.

It is better to express how a person's behavior affected you or made you *feel,* rather than your being "right" or their being "wrong." This puts the focus on the relationship and connection that exists between you and the other person, rather than judgments of behaviors as right or wrong.

If a past conflict keeps coming up, it has most likely not been resolved, or the resulting agreements were not actually agreed upon by both people. Holding on to feelings of resentment or bitterness only perpetuates the conflict. If there is retaliation during or after the conflict resolution process is complete with the intent of punishing, then obviously this has the potential to destroy any progress made. Being able to let go of resolved conflicts without

204

hanging on to residual feelings allows relationships to move forward. Acts of kindness and love are what we remember over time, not the conflicts we negotiated. Navigating conflicts with honor and respect enhances our ability to resolve future conflicts and brings the trust and peace of mind that comes from knowing both people in a relationship have the ability and willingness to resolve conflicts effectively.

Apologies

If there are any actions, words or behaviors during a conflict that were intentionally hurtful or harmful, then apologize! Apologizing won't always remove the scars of hurt, but an apology lessens the pain. Apologizing doesn't mean that you are necessarily right or wrong. It means that you value the relationship more than you value your need to be right. If someone needs to apologize to you and has not, then ask that person for an apology, or at least for acknowledgement the conflict has occurred. Conflict resolution may begin or end with an apology and has the following benefits:

- ✓ An apology tells you and the other person that you are mature enough to be vulnerable and accept responsibility for your actions, even when they are not always right.
- ✓ Apologizing shows the other person you respect and care about the relationship and are willing to offer your words of personal responsibility to clear the air and move forward.
- ✓ Apologizing for your part of the conflict shows you are *Adult* enough to take full responsibility for your words, actions, or behaviors.
- ✓ An apology has the added benefit of opening the door to allow the other person to apologize for any hurtful or inappropriate words or actions on their part.

An unsolicited apology carries the greatest weight, but the next best apology is a solicited apology.

The timeliness of an apology indicates the other person's sincerity and regard for the relationship. For example, if an apology is received for a serious conflict that occurred a year ago, the apology helps to resolve any residual hurt or resentment. Had the apology been received at the time of the conflict, then no residual hurt or resentment may have developed. Don't wait to resolve conflicts if you have had time to get clear on your responsibility in a conflict and what, if any, apology is needed by you. This means the time to apologize is at most days after the need is clear—not weeks, months, or years.

Acknowledging apologies is just as important as giving them. If you do not acknowledge a received apology, chances are you haven't accepted the apology and are still harboring unresolved feelings of resentment. If this occurs, ask yourself what is unresolved and why the apology is not enough, or what would bring resolution. If possible, bring these issues back to the conflict resolution process for negotiation. If apologies are not acknowledged, feelings of resentment, distrust, or hurt can develop and deepen.

An apology should always fit the level of injury or damage that occurred. Sometimes it may be as simple as, "I'm sorry," and other times the apology could include a nice written card or note expressing your regret or sorrow, or a gift or flowers. If you feel the words "I'm sorry" negate who you are or do not convey exactly what you feel, then state more explicitly what exactly you are apologizing for through words or actions.

Apologies are not always necessary, and are not always the resolution needed. An apology may help, but there can also be a need for more discussion of feelings that occurred during the conflict by one or both people, or discussion of new agreements, boundaries, or commitments going forward. It is always good to acknowledge another person's feelings, whether you agree with that person or not. You can make statements like, "I understand you feel this way." Acknowledging another person's feelings shows you care, and that you are trying to understand them. It is not necessary to ingratiate yourself to another by going beyond acknowledgment, apology and personal responsibility to receive their forgiveness.

Sometimes words of apology are not enough. Taking responsibility may also mean making amends through actions or behaviors that go beyond an "I'm sorry" statement of apology. If the apology is for bad or hurtful behavior intended to change, then an accompanying commitment of the intended changes should be clearly stated with the apology. For an apology to lead to any change in behavior there must be an understanding of what the apology is for, or there is a high probability that the offending behavior will be repeated. Repeated apologies for hurtful behaviors or actions, without taking responsibility to change the offending behavior or action, are nothing but idle words.

An apology can be perceived as a sign of weakness or an attempt to hold the person apologizing indebted. This stops the healing process that occurs with an apology and makes the person apologizing less likely to apologize in the future. An apology is always best given graciously when it is required and graciously acknowledged when received.

Sometimes to get a relationship back on track, words need to be spoken that are truthful, yet painful. However, if the words or accusations are not completely truthful or are intended to hurt, then apologize and acknowledge which are untrue or inappropriate. Constructive criticism delivered in a way that is loving and helpful is always better than criticism that comes across as harsh or judgmental.

We all need to use the phrases 'Thank You', 'I'm sorry', 'I take full responsibility for my part.', 'I forgive you' and 'I love you' much more often. These phrases are both healing and cathartic in their ability to move our relationships forward. These simple phrases used sincerely help us to resolve conflicts, heal past hurts and sustain healthy relationships.

***

Managing Expectations

Expectations can be the source of conflicts in our relationships, especially if they are unfair, or we feel they are not being met. Either way, something has to change, and the first and easiest step is to look honestly at our personal expectations of others and continually ask if they are fair and reasonable. Our expectations of others are usually centered on our needs for another's resources such as time, money, energy, or particular behaviors. Conflicts can occur when expectations for these resources are not clearly verbalized, known, fair, or reasonable. When we clearly communicate our expectations, we can get clear commitment from everyone involved or negotiate an agreeable solution for resources. Managing the expectations of others starts with you getting clear in your communication about what you desire, what you can or cannot do, what your expectations are, and what your true feelings are in relationship to the other person. Resentment arises when we have unfulfilled expectations, or we have over-given and not received in return. To remove resentment related to expectation, either remove or modify the expectation or limit over giving.

One way we can over-give is by making life too convenient or easy for another at the expense of our own convenience and ease of living. When we consciously decide not to meet the expectations of another and clearly communicate this, then any resulting behavior that is negative or persecuting in nature is unacceptable. Examples of these residual behaviors might include trying to make you feel guilty, abusive or hurtful language, or pulling away because the other person did not get their way. The following questions can be useful when managing personal expectations of another person.

- ✓ Is the expectation fair and reasonable for this relationship?
- ✓ Is the expectation reciprocal, or is there a double standard in place for either party?
- ✓ Was there adequate time given to meet the expectation?
- ✓ Was the expectation clear, either verbally or in writing?

✓ In the big picture, is the expectation something significant or insignificant?

✓ Can you shift your perspective of what is needed and/or drop the expectation if the other person cannot, will not, or is not able to meet your expectation?

Always give a person the time or space to make the right choice or do the right thing, without projecting what you think they should do, or penalizing them up front because you believe they won't meet your expectations. Always come from a place of positive expectation that the right choice will be made, without projecting negative assumptions or false beliefs. Our skill at accepting the unexpected is essential when it comes to managing our expectations of others.

Engaging the process of managing expectations does not insure outcomes will go as we like or as we expect. As humans we behave and respond differently in each moment. In relationship to others, the only control we have is how we choose to respond, our ability to shift our personal perspective, and how we choose to go forward in relationship. You will set yourself up continually to experience loss, if your expectations of others are unfair, unreasonable, or not known. It is normal to experience disappointment when expectations are not met or fulfilled, but when we carry these disappointments with us for months or years, this clearly becomes emotionally unhealthy and affects the relationship involved. Forgiveness helps us get over our disappointments with others. Forgiveness does not condone the behavior or diminish the disappointment, but it frees us from carrying disappointment arising from failed expectations forward throughout our lives. Extreme disappointment we carry or continually "replay" may require a trained professional or therapist to assist us in the process of letting go.

Responsible *Adults* are present in their interactions and understand the importance of effectively managing expectations of themselves and others. They know what they want and clearly communicate these needs and expectations to others. This clarity removes ambiguity and provides full transparency in relationships that sustain them. Managing our expectations of others or their expectations of us helps to minimize unnecessary conflicts.

Negotiation

We are always in a process of negotiation when engaged with other people, whether negotiation is obvious or not. There is always something you need from someone else, or something someone needs from you. Learning to negotiate effectively provides a rich life experience in which our reasonable needs are met while unnecessary conflicts are avoided in the process.

Good negotiation skills become a preemptive way of resolving conflicts before they occur. Our objections to the way others behave come from the gray area between what we desire and what another is willing to provide. Learning to negotiate up front for what we want and need prevents our objections from escalating into unwanted conflicts.

The negotiation process is a series of mutual agreements we make to achieve agreeable outcomes. Negotiation requires asking for what we want in a fair and reasonable manner. Fair negotiation requires a process of give and take (also called give/get) allowing for the possibility that both people's needs are met, and both can walk away feeling win/win.

The negotiation process begins when one or both sides clearly ask for what they desire. The negotiation process continues by giving in some areas and conceding in other areas until a mutually beneficial agreement is reached. This process involves going back and forth with "I will give this, if I can get that" until all areas of negotiation are satisfied. There are continual gives and takes until no more are required or until final agreement is reached. If giving becomes one-sided, it betrays the negotiation process, because the person taking too much appears to desire only their gain, and this betrays the trust of the person doing all the giving. Responding during the negotiation process with unfair expectations, bullying, or the connecting of services to other expectations can be damaging to the negotiation process as well.

Another key to successful negotiation is to keep negotiating until you reach either an agreement and there is fair resolution for one or both parties, or you agree to stop negotiating. Negotiating outcomes too quickly can cause making agreements that might be considered mistakes later. If the negotiation process feels rushed or hurried, then slow the process down to give yourself time to figure out your next response or your next counter-offer.

Keep focused on the results desired during negotiating without getting your ego involved, and work toward a win-win situation for all involved if possible. If a negotiation becomes overly charged or emotional, then step away and return when everyone is able to proceed calmly. Be flexible to give in some areas and assertive enough to ask for what you want in other areas.

Understand your motivations in the negotiating process, and the motivations of other people. What do they want, and why do they want it? What do you want, and why do you want it? Learning to see what a person's position is in the negotiation process and their motivation helps to facilitate the negotiation. It is important to understand if you or the other person wants money, time, power, resources, control, or simply to win. For both people to feel as though they have won in the negotiation process, neither party can give too much or take too much.

Negotiation requires people step into an intimate relationship with one another, even if only for the short period of time it takes to negotiate a solution. This means both people are willing to be somewhat vulnerable and share their needs and concerns honestly.

All parties involved should enter into the negotiation process in good faith, which means conducting the negotiation in a fair, reasonable, and transparent manner. Negotiating in good faith is being honest about what you will do and what you won't do during the negotiation process. This honesty clears up ambiguity and allows everyone to go forward making the most informed decision they can with the facts presented for their desired outcomes. Transparency provides the means for full disclosure of what is being negotiated, how it is negotiated, and the associated reasons for the negotiation, as well as full accountability for the decisions made during the negotiation process.

Negotiating in a fair and respectful manner is important to prevent the negotiation from becoming overly emotional. Degrading another person or their resources to try and gain an advantage is a negative way to approach negotiation and often causes the process to fail.

It is important to learn to negotiate well, for negotiation can avoid disagreements that lead to conflicts. If done well, negotiation is one of our greatest tools in navigating life and relationships in a peaceful and harmonious way as responsible *Adults*.

The Standoff Conflict

A conflict becomes unresolved when either there is no awareness a conflict occurred, or one or both parties are unwilling to take any responsibility for the conflict, the necessary first step in resolving a conflict. When a conflict occurs and there is no movement by either party toward resolution, then a standoff results. Either party can take the first step in conflict resolution, but it is most honorable when the person with most culpability steps up first to initiate the conflict resolution process.

It is always important to remember that most people do not have adequate conflict resolution skills. Reading these sections on conflict resolution will equip you better than most and provide the awareness of the first steps toward conflict resolution. If either the negotiation process or conflict resolution skills are broken in a relationship, then these must first be repaired so the relationship can get back on track. The ability to resolve a conflict usually breaks down when there is a breach of trust. Repairing and reestablishing reciprocal trust is the solution to get effective conflict resolution and negotiation back on track.

When conflicts do not resolve, then depending on the severity and scope of the conflict, decisions must be made about how to proceed in the relationship. Whether the conflict is large or small, time that goes on without resolution is damaging to the relationship. Unresolved conflicts can leave behind an energy that can continue to build more energy that eventually precipitates another conflict, and so the cycle continues. On the other hand, if the relationship is valued enough, time can heal insignificant conflicts, and they can become irrelevant and easily forgiven. Large conflicts can be negotiated if both parties remain willing to forgive and engage to find mutually satisfying outcomes through honest and open dialogue.

People who do not have conflict resolution skills may leave a conflict or avoid attempts at reconciliation and resolution. Not responding to requests to resolve conflict can be perceived as passive aggressive behavior. In extreme situations in which people do not know how to resolve conflicts, a conflict may cause a response of anger or complete desertion in order to avoid having to deal with the conflict. Anger and additional drama can be a way to deflect attention away from the conflict or its true cause. Any of these types of avoidance tactics are usually employed because the people involved do not want to resolve the conflict, are not comfortable with conflict resolution, or do not have the skills to resolve conflicts.

A person's ability to resolve conflicts can be one of their greatest strengths or greatest weaknesses. Our history is filled with conflicts resolved through war and destruction, because leaders could not resolve conflicts with truth, integrity, and a mastery of diplomacy. One example of a leader with a great ability for conflict resolution was Mahatma Gandhi, who turned conflict in India into independence for a nation through his commitment to non-violence, truth, and freedom for all people.

Wars arising out of our inability to resolve conflicts have killed untold millions of people who either felt forced to fight for what they believed in or were innocent bystanders to the ravages of war. If the time, money, and energy spent on war is invested in finding viable solutions to conflicts that cause war, there might be a chance for peace on this planet.

Becoming a responsible *Adult* requires stepping into a role in which we deal with conflict directly and are willing to do our part to resolve conflicts with the best possible outcome for all involved. The process of conflict resolution will serve you and those around you to maintain and sustain peaceful relationships.

CHAPTER TWELVE

When Relationships End

Relationships end when one or both parties are not getting their needs or expectations fulfilled, and one or both no longer experience peace and happiness. It takes two people to sustain a relationship but one person alone can cause a relationship to fail. There can be natural reasons for a relationship to end such as the distance that moving away creates and subsequent energy it requires to sustain, or reasons resulting from behaviors that no longer serve healthy encounters in the relationship. It can be easy to give up and stop trying in a relationship and walk away; the more difficult task is to stay in the relationship, resolve conflicts, create healthy boundaries and create a healthier paradigm for how to interact. It is more often the case that relationships do not need to end if what is needed, or what is not needed are honored by both people. What is needed by the relationship is best requested directly and honestly and given the time to fulfill. What is not needed by the relationship requires mutual agreements of healthy boundaries that are respected and maintained.

The first question to ask when there are unmet expectations and a relationship is failing is "Are my needs and expectations fair and reasonable?" The second question is "Can this person fulfill all of those needs and expectations?" If the individual cannot fulfill these fair expectations, do you want to stay in the relationship, and are you willing to do the work it takes to get the relationship back to a healthy place? Are your differences/problems solvable? When life becomes too difficult or demanding, time apart is sometimes all that is needed. If either party is unwilling to do the work required to get the relationship back on track, or is unwilling to take time apart before doing the work needed to get back on track, then it is probably best to move on. However, every consideration

215

should be made to work out problems, as many times we end old relationships only to find ourselves in new relationships with the same pattern of issues, problems or unfulfilled expectations that need to be resolved. No betrayal or breach of trust is insurmountable in a relationship if both parties are willing to engage in the *Six Keys to Conflict Resolution*, create healthy boundaries and recommit to harmony through the *Ten Elements of Healthy Relationships*.

The Signs of a Failing Relationship

It is often hard to recognize the signs of a failing relationship, and even when the signs are present it does not always mean a relationship needs to end. These signs may just mean readjustment or refocus is needed to get the relationship back on track. Readjustment occurs through setting new boundaries, making new commitments, or incorporating changes in behavior. Any relationship that no longer brings joy and peace to your life is probably over and best let go. It takes energy to maintain a relationship that no longer brings love and happiness or even the desire to engage. Time compounds this overextension of your energy and leads to resentment if the situation is not addressed. There is a tendency to stay with what we know, even when doing so is unhealthy or makes us unhappy. Not every relationship is destined to make it to the end of our life. We make room for more meaningful relationships when we remove the extraneous relationships that no longer serve us or bring meaning to our lives.

You can see the signs of a relationship ending by noticing how two people engage and by observing their overall happiness. Are they joyful in each other's presence? Or, is joy only expressed to other people or only when other people are present? Another sign a relationship is failing is evident when there is little or no desire to be in that person's presence, and interactions become less frequent and/or less intimate. Minor differences or unresolved conflicts may explode into major arguments resulting from buildup of tension in the relationship. There may be unexplained outbursts of

216

anger, unfair expectations or boundaries placed on the relationship. Continual bickering or argument over small or large details that do not get resolved can also indicate problems remaining unaddressed and in need of attention.

When hurt arises in any separation, so too may drama or dysfunction. This drama and dysfunction is often used consciously or unconsciously to distract from the actual issues needing resolution, or to facilitate the separation more easily by one or both parties. Taking a more direct approach supersedes the need to engage in drama or dysfunction to bring about separation.

The reasons for ending relationships may vary widely, but a serious betrayal or repeated failure of commitments are often the causes. Healthy relationships require trust and intimacy for their sustenance, and any breakdown in trust is experienced as betrayal. When betrayal occurs, resentment and distrust can be the resulting feelings. Resentment, distrust, and feelings of betrayal may combine to indicate a failing relationship.

Once betrayal is identified, failure to have open and honest communication adds to the detriment of the relationship. Open and honest communication will allow the resolution of conflicts and problems to occur, and without this communication, probably doom. Every relationship will endure conflicts, and our willingness to resolve conflicts, even conflicts of betrayal, determines how our relationships proceed. Resentment can be one of the hardest issues to work through, because the mind attaches to and continuously replays the source of its resentment. If either party has feelings of resentment, these feelings must be brought forward so they can be looked at, discussed openly, and resolved. Complete conflict resolution allows the relationship to start again from a new point of forgiveness, agreement, and commitment. Without conflict resolution or unreconciled differences, relationships come to their logical conclusion.

Staying in relationships that are dysfunctional, unhealthy, or have unresolved conflicts can cause additional problems over time. There are

217

people who remain loyal to a relationship even though the relationship has digressed into negative patterns of failed commitments or needs that are no longer met. Loyalty is hugely important in a long-term relationship, but its importance can fade when the idea of loyalty is all there is keeping the relationship together. Loyalty for loyalties sake won't solve some of the hard issues like failed commitments, lack of intimacy, lost love, or lost connection. Both parties must be willing to step up and own their part of a failed relationship, and then be willing to work to make it better or courageously admit the relationship failed. The greatest challenge may be when you no longer love someone and find yourself together merely out of convenience or for the fear of moving apart or being alone.

A relationship that no longer brings joy or love to your life eventually takes too much energy to sustain and can lead to emotional suffering and even eventual physical illness and disease. Repressing one's true feelings or harboring resentment can gradually erode the ability to interact in the relationship in a healthy way, eventually causing the relationship to end.

When trying to salvage a relationship, there are several options to consider: All of them must eventually involve the effective communication of needs, desires, and expectations, and the resolution of any unresolved conflicts. If the relationship has suffered long term, each of these areas must be identified and a plan made for discussion, resolution, and the creation of new agreements, which will in turn lead to new commitments.

Rather than ending a relationship, a cooling off period might also be considered, with the intention of coming back together later to resolve differences. This time allows both people to consider their parts in any conflict that has occurred and to resolve any intense feelings of hurt or anger. The cooling off period may encourage the willingness to come back together and resolve differences at a later date.

There is no need to engage friends and family in choosing sides or making judgments when relationships end. This un-adult behavior can become unconstructive, divisive and serves no one well. Relationships are

218

best measured through direct engagement and not through hearsay and conjecture. All too often friends and family choose sides or step out of your life completely because of their judgment or resultant hurt feelings. In the process of choosing sides, lies or partial truths can be told to make the other party in a relationship look bad, so support can be garnered for the person telling the untruths. Be supportive of people who are going through rough stages in their relationships and avoid being judgmental of either person in the relationship. Difficulties in relationships are ultimately the business of the two people going through the challenging times together, not anyone else.

In any relationship, the most loving thing you can do for another person is to set them free; and give them permission to be who they are without your projections of who you want them to be. Truly loving someone is to completely set that person free to be who they are at any point in time. This freedom means sometimes we become closer and more intimate, and sometimes we grow in different directions or apart, but either way— freedom is the true north in relationships.

Rejection

Rejection occurs when who we are or what we offer is not accepted, and we experience feelings of non-acceptance or exclusion. When a relationship ends or changes in dynamics, such as moving from a romance to a friendship, or from a friend to a casual acquaintance, one or both parties can experience feelings of rejection. Just like any intense emotion, rejection feels intense initially and then gradually lessens and subsides. Time truly does heal us, and allowing ourselves to experience our feelings fully without repression greatly helps the process of healing feelings of rejection. Also, when we stop giving an emotion more energy with continual thoughts about it, the emotion has a chance to heal more quickly. Getting caught up in feelings of personal rejection can become immobilizing. Healing sets us free.

People are not willing to go forward in relationships for thousands of reasons; most have to do with personal desires and preferences that have no connection with the person being rejected. Personal preferences and desires are simply that: personal preferences and desires. Trying to change to accommodate a person's preferences or desires, or expecting another person to change to meet your preferences or desires, is a common mistake in relationships. If there is something you need to change and are willing to change, try to make the change on your own and see if that works for you. If it does not work, seek professional advice to help you make the change

If there is something about your intrinsic being you are being asked or expected to change, then the other person's expectations of you are out of alignment and unfair. Asking anyone to change who they are, or to become someone based on expectations that are unfair, arbitrary, or unreasonable, limits a person's freedom and places an unnecessary burden on them and the relationship. A healthy relationship asks that we always be fair and reciprocal in our expectations of another person and not expect them to change in areas intrinsic to their being.

For example, if a body type is heavy-set, and a person wants a leaner partner, then this expectation is unfair and cannot be fulfilled by a heavy-set person. If a person likes quiet and introverted people, then being with a loud extrovert does not work. We cannot be expected to change intrinsic parts of our being, including physical attributes, personality traits, or behaviors that are core to our being. Negative behaviors may be changeable over time, however not without the initial awareness these behaviors exist and there is desire to change. There must also be a willingness to admit change is needed, as well as a true willingness to make change happen.

Everyone experiences rejection in a relationship at some point in his or her life. Rejection may ultimately be our protection against whatever does not serve our highest good. If rejection occurs too early in a relationship, it may eliminate the possibility for a friendship. If the relationship is to go forward in the form of friendship, then obviously how the rejection is delivered is critical. For example, if the rejection is inherently about physical looks, then this shows a focus on superficial qualities only and may eliminate the potential to move forward based on the more important inner qualities as friends. If rejection is done with respect, based on personal interests or desires that are non-judgmental, no one can argue or find fault with these reasons.

We will all experience times of acceptance and times of rejection throughout our lives. When it comes to college, you might not make the cut for the best schools. When it comes to dating, you won't be the perfect partner for everyone. When it comes to friends, your gift of friendship won't be valued by everyone. You also won't be qualified for every job that you apply for. Rejection is a part of life that requires we learn to accept, to let go, and to continue to love ourselves. If we do not learn to deal with rejection, life can begin to seem hostile, unfriendly, unfair, and unkind. In reality, these feelings are ultimately only our beliefs, our lack of acceptance, and our inability to deal with rejection effectively. Learning to deal with rejection is about coming to accept ourselves, and the fact that we may not always be wanted or accepted by everyone.

Dealing effectively with rejection is about learning to recognize what you have the power to change, what you do not have the power to change, and the wisdom to know the difference. You can either accept what you cannot change or be willing to do the work to make the changes within your self. Dealing with rejection then becomes a natural part of life, and you feel comfortable with who you are and what you offer to the world and to other people. Rejection becomes a time of introspection and then a movement forward in a healthy manner and new direction.

We must learn to love ourselves as we are and where we are in our lives, so our foundation of confidence is neither shaken, nor destroyed, when we face rejections in life. If you are being rejected for something about yourself that cannot be changed, why would you in any way feel hurt, attacked, or dejected? How or why would you change something intrinsically you? If you are being rejected because of traits you can change but are unwilling to

221

change, your decision is still an acceptable choice. It is always wise to give another person the opportunity or the time they need to accept you as you are.

In the case of dating, if someone says "I don't like your body odor," then you can try taking more frequent showers. In the case of a job, if someone states you do not have either the experience or the education they are looking for, then you can decide to seek out schooling and experience with other companies. If changing something about yourself feels too complex or unreasonable, then it probably is, and you can decide if you truly want to change it at all.

Becoming an *Adult* is learning how to manifest our dreams and desires in our lives. The people who are really successful at life are the ones who can hear "No" hundreds of times and yet keep pursuing their dreams and desires until they get a "Yes." Success is often born from the process of moving from one failure to another failure and learning from our mistakes, until the process teaches us what is needed for our final success to unfold.

Grow comfortable and confident with the person you are, and believe in yourself enough so rejections become fine adjustments along your path to becoming more you. Let the process lead you into more success and realization of your dreams, not into tsunami waves of regret.

Alone

There are both physical and mental aspects of being alone. The mental concept of "aloneness" is a construct we create when we believe we are separate from ourselves or separate from others. The concept of aloneness often gets supported through modern media and the beliefs of others that portray a world where being alone does not exist, or is somehow unhealthy for us. How do we reconnect with our true selves and see all of the love existing within us, around us, and for us? How do we deconstruct the idea that there even exists a state of "alone"? How do we define ourselves without the need to be defined by others or outside influences?

It can be very useful to inquire directly into any experience of aloneness. What does it mean to be alone, and what would it mean to not be alone? Does being alone mean a lack of physical proximity to another person? Does it mean we are not heard and no one listens? Does it mean we feel disconnected from others? Are our connections meaningless or lacking intimacy? Does time with others dictate whether or not we are alone? Does the connection or intimacy we experience when we are with others impact our feelings of aloneness or togetherness?

When we understand our true nature as that which is already abiding everywhere and in everything, the awareness begins to dawn that we are never truly alone, and our ego has used this belief construct of "alone" as a means of separation from ourselves. With this said, there are people who live physically alone or separated from others, and their aloneness is a source of sadness, not joy. If we cannot be physically alone, then life will present as very lonely, because most of our time is spent alone with ourselves.

We are taught to seek validation and self-worth through relationships with other people, and through the belief that acceptance by others will make us feel less alone, complete or whole. Can we be in acceptance of ourselves completely? Can we be complete and whole without identifying ourselves through others? Can we be in a relationship with ourselves and be fulfilled? The answer is yes, although human relationships, pets, and contact with others also provide us a sense of the connection and belonging we seek.

For the most part, the belief in aloneness arises from a society in which too much emphasis is placed on being in a relationship, romantic or otherwise, with too much expectation that our happiness is dependent only on our relationships with others, rather than looking at the quality of those relationships, or the important relationship we have with our self. Living alone has become a viable option for those who have the financial means and do not desire to share living arrangements with others. While the higher costs of living may require many more of us to live together communally, living alone is explored here as a viable choice for those who can live simply.

Communal living not only allows sharing domestic work, but also the sharing of the communal living experience.

A growing percentage of individuals today are choosing to live alone and doing so happily. Living alone can be a happy life if we are content with the relationship with ourselves and content with living alone. One choice becomes clear: live alone rather than be subservient to those who would inhibit or limit your progress or your peace of mind.

If we are constantly pining for a relationship or to share our lives with another, then living alone won't be an enjoyable or joyful experience. A part of living alone is learning to become content to enjoy life without the expectation that someone else is responsible for our happiness. This has the added effect of teaching us to love ourselves more. Too often we look outside ourselves for happiness or to other people to validate our self-worth. Learning that we have intrinsic value sets us free to live alone or with others, without the belief that we are somehow lacking or incomplete without another at our side.

Our beliefs about being alone can determine our happiness. Often this requires we let go of any belief there is an "alone," and to see this is simply a negative belief that prevents us from enjoying our time alone in relationship with ourselves. We can believe there is something missing from our lives or there is something unfulfilled. If this is the case, then figure out what you want or need to fulfill. If you believe living alone is akin to being an outcast, or something sad or tragic, then your time living alone will feel sad, tragic, and lonely. If you believe your time alone can be fulfilling, and you feel the joy of having experiences of your own, then you will find this time rewarding and joyful.

When living alone, you always have yourself, and beyond *you* it helps to have close friends who check in or with whom you can spend social time. There are always ways to engage with other people daily through friendships, work relationships, and casual relationships. Outside of working or having a job, having something to look forward to while living alone gives purpose and meaning for the future and keeps us engaged in the process of life.

In general, humans are communal beings who like to live with or near other humans. A life filled with the richness of healthy relationships is a life filled with happiness and joy. Living alone is a viable option, but at the end of each day, someone who cares about where we were or what we did, and shares this information with us can bring more joy, satisfaction and a sense of belonging to each day. Our connection to ourselves and to others brings meaning to our lives, and we are each personally responsible for defining that meaning. We come in to this life alone and will leave this life alone. How we fill the time in between with meaningful relationships, both with ourselves and with others, defines our happiness.

CONCLUSION

Deepening Our Connection

I f ever there was a time in human history, now is the time we must come together on this planet to form deeper bonds and connections in our relationships to insure our survival. We cannot solve the problems of the world without developing resilient and sustainable relationships that bring us back into balance with ourselves and with nature. Achieving this requires we explore in depth the needs of the human ego, while at the same time we supersede egoic need with the realization of our inherent connection to all living beings on this planet. We can no longer only take care of ourselves: we have to take care of all of life on this planet.

Ultimately, we all want freedom to live our lives, but with seven billion people on this planet and a finite amount of space and limited resources, a shift in our ability to resolve and negotiate conflicts is needed. Each of us must be free to be the person or being we were put here to be, and to allow all of life this same freedom, negotiating needs, boundaries and conflicts as they arise. The most loving gift we can give another person in any relationship is the freedom and permission to be who they are without our judgment, control, or unsolicited input. The people who in return set us free and respect our needs and boundaries become life's most cherished relationships. An important measure of our happiness is how free we are in our relationships, and how free we feel to have our desired experiences both individually and together.

Our connections to family, friends, communities, and cultures on this planet have become less and less important, while the engines of capitalism drive societies to support corporations instead of the totality of life and what will support our human experience going forward. Sharing and compromise will comprise the new world order, or chaos, squander, and consumption will

226

prevail. We must deepen our connections to each other by reestablishing patterns of generosity, honesty, gratitude, reciprocity, and integrity in all of our relationships. We must also strengthen our connections through deeper intimacy, healthy boundaries, conflict resolution, and removal of drama and dysfunction. Our quality of life depends on the quality of our connections to all of life. No one can be left out; no one can be excluded; no one can be judged of less value or unworthy. Our differences must be viewed as expressions of diversity, unique and interesting, and not the basis for judgmentalism or separation. Without deeper connections there is continued movement toward separation, isolation, and exclusion.

We are individually responsible for bringing our own life into order i.e. free of drama and dysfunction with self-love and self-respect. Once this personal order is established, an energy is available to us in alignment with harmony that allows us to show up with healthy abundance in our relationships.

Our relationships have the potential to bring rich experiences of connection with others that establish meaning and purpose in our lives. Without these connections and the very real sense of belonging to a community, we feel isolated and as though something is missing from our lives. We search for meaning and purpose through more technology, more distractions, and addictions that serve only to dumb us down, rather than awaken us to our true being. We thrive through our connections to others and weaken without them.

Our relationships bring us opportunities to choose better and do better in all interactions. Raising our awareness through self-observation of the dynamics of relationships, and how they can serve us in healthy and not so healthy ways, offers us the opportunity to change our relationship to ourselves, and how we interact with others: changes which can bring peace and happiness to all our relationships. However, the peace and happiness we achieve cannot be at the expense of causing others to suffer or bringing misery to others.

Depending on where you were when you started reading this book, you will begin to incorporate changes resulting from your new understanding of what you have read and discovered here, leading to a shift in your awareness. Once your awareness shifts, you will begin to incorporate corresponding behaviors that match your new awareness, leading to personal change. Getting out of drama and dysfunction in relationships and incorporating healthy relationship dynamics is one more step toward *Adult* awareness, and one more step toward our personal evolution.

Personal behavioral change is a gradual process taking both time and patience. These types of changes usually occur with big "Ahaa" moments that take you three steps forward, and then can be followed by reverting to old behaviors that take you two steps backward. The end result, however, is greater awareness of how to live a more fulfilling and peaceful life, an awareness that is always being gained one step forward at a time. Even though we may know intellectually that we are engaged in unhealthy patterns previously perceived as loving, we will keep engaging in these until we become aware of these patterns and then make changes. Awareness takes us halfway there, incorporating the change into permanence is the full distance.

As we continually increase our awareness of the elements that nurture and sustain healthy relationships and those that lead us into unhealthy relationships, we can make conscious choices in how we attract and retain relationships that are resilient and serve our higher good. Observing our interactions and the resulting outcomes is all the experience needed to cultivate healthy dynamics and behaviors that serve relationships in healthy ways. Conscious awareness can result in anything from detached observation to engaged participation, but ultimately supports our making more informed choices. With the power of choice comes personal responsibility for all of our actions and behaviors in relationships.

Empathy and awareness cannot be taught, but they can increase through life experiences, or through meditation practices during which we cultivate empathy and genuine prayer for the betterment and evolution of all beings.

228

Our experiences can teach us all we need to learn when we engage in a regular practice of self-observation. We all have the potential to share in universal awareness that is always present. This awareness is continually setting up life experiences for us—considered bad or good, but really neither—to achieve the goal of complete awareness. Observation is all that is required.

Empathy and compassion are measures of our ability to feel for other people, but also our ability to understand other people and find common ground for healthier relationships. Whereas judgmentalism and jealousy separates and isolates, empathy and compassion bring us better understanding and awareness of others, ultimately bringing us closer together.

Continually developing our empathy for all living beings on this planet, not just humans, is what allows us to step out of the thought patterns of judgment, jealousy, and anger that diminish our overall capacity for empathy and cause separation. These patterns may arise from our past experiences, both positive and negative, which we carry into each relationship and corresponding interactions. As we continually raise our self-awareness of healthier paradigms for engaging with others, we can remain strong in the moment and respond with choices that keep us grounded in our newfound awareness of sustainable methods to relate with one another. Each relationship needs revisiting to reveal drama or dysfunctional behaviors and needs periodic adjustments to eliminate those behaviors that no longer serve us. Drama and dysfunction are patterns of behavior that become addictive for some, requiring time and energy to sustain and time and energy to release. This reevaluation process gives all of our relationships the respect, care, and support they require to become healthier. Some relationships willingly engage in new and healthy ways, while others will resist and potentially need new boundaries established, to suspend or end. Eventually, we become responsible *Adults* when we step into our true selves, live from our hearts and step out of dysfunctional behaviors and relationships that no longer serve us.

Once you begin to observe the relationship dynamics around you, you may realize how far you have come, and how others are stuck in repetitive patterns of un-adult behaviors. The goal is not to become judgmental of others from any new level of awareness attained, but rather to attain a higher state where you experience people with empathy for where they are in their journey without feeling the need to judge or change them. Your awareness allows you to see clearly how to interact with others for the most positive outcome for you and for them, and when this is not possible you are able to set respectful boundaries to maintain your ongoing peace and happiness.

As we establish a greater intimacy with ourselves we naturally begin to experience more intimate connections to all of life. In the spiritual sense, this intimacy within ourselves can be termed "awakening to oneness." We develop personal intimacy with others by first reconnecting our hearts with our thoughts and emotions, and then communicating these outward with our utmost honesty and vulnerability. Deepening intimate connections in existing relationships and developing intimacy in new relationships will serve to provide the depth of connections we seek.

Finally, we can extend intimacy to the communities in which we live by interacting with true authenticity and integrity, providing real solutions to problems, rather than bringing our egoic problems to the table in need of solutions. Intimacy becomes the law of attraction that brings back connection, meaning, and purpose to all of our relationships.

Resilient World Communities

From our individual bonds of intimacy, a network of intimacy can extend outward through which we are able to form resilient communities. Family can bring structure and connections we seek, but a whole community of acceptance, tolerance and extended families builds the foundation for a successful society. While intimacy starts with family, it must extend out into our communities, where we treat everyone as family regardless of race, sexual preference, religion, or politics. Shifting our perception to see we are all "one of us" in this world community helps develop the unity we seek and

230

ultimately will sustain humankind on this planet. We need to create world communities that express global intimacy. Global intimacy exists when different cultures seek to understand one another and embrace their differences and diversity, rather than separate from each other and create boundaries and wars over their differences and boundaries. The time is now for a redesign of humankind, both how we think individually, and how we think and interact with each other collectively and with the world around us.

There is need right now to revisit the ideas of villages within our communities in which people not only know each other, but also care and support each other through simple acts of showing up when needed for every inhabitant. A collective breakdown in community structure occurs when people are excluded, judged, and made to feel separate: all failures in the intimacy fibers that connect us. Everyone must be included, everyone must participate, and everyone must do his or her part to create this fabric of connectivity, like links in a chain, or the entire structure fails at the weakest links. A shared vision and goal for each village, one that supports individuals, will bring all people together in communities under a shared goal of sustainable relationships that connect to form a resilient world community.

While we pass on great achievements in the arts and sciences from one generation to the next, we have not learned the lessons of past societies regarding what led them to war and what led them to peace. How we define our relationships among people, cultures, and nations going forward determines how we are to peacefully coexist or how we will degrade into destructive conflict. History is rich with teachings of how we can coexist on this planet to create new socially responsible cultures that resolve conflicts, not create them.

Our differences across countries, races, and cultures can be viewed as opportunities for acceptance of diversity, not as a means to increase separation. We are all alone in the sense that each one of us is having a personal life experience and an individual evolution, but we are always connected to everyone and everything, and reestablishing those connections

231

is needed now more than ever. Relationships will always provide challenges that offer opportunities for growth and evolution providing we adapt the skills required to navigate differences, expectations, conflicts, and hurts. Healing our relationships requires we remember this very simple connectedness to everyone at all times.

To be a contributing force of good in the world means reaching a level of awareness that allows us to see our relationship to ourselves and everyone else with equality. It means respecting fair boundaries, developing intimacy with others through our honesty and vulnerability, showing up when needed for the greater good of those involved, and managing conflicts respectfully with win-win resolutions while staying out of drama and dysfunction.

The survival of our species and our planet now depends on our ability to connect more authentically to one another, not less. This deepening connection is the groundwork for building sustainable systems that support a global community that nurtures and cares for one another, not just the few with one defined currency. It takes many types of currencies to rebuild and sustain healthy communities built on compromise, commitments, reciprocity, trust, and support. Each individual is that link, that connection, in the chain of human experience and evolution. Each of us can EVOLVE a new human experience.

The dynamics of healthy relationship found here in the first book of EVOLVE has given you a means by which to engage in new, healthier paradigms, and a basis for understanding what it means to show up as a true *Adult* in all our relationships. From here on out, each of your relationship experiences is an opportunity to step into the very real state of *Adult*hood and to step out of those behaviors limiting your potential to be all you can be and to live a life of true peace, happiness, and inner fulfillment.

While we all want to have healthy relationships all of the time, we can only start to incorporate the ideas found here over time, and then observe our progress forward with each successful interaction, each resolved conflict, and each step out of dysfunction and unnecessary drama. Continually raising your awareness in the key areas of healthy relationships and experiencing what harmony feels like with others and the world helps achieve personal balance and fulfillment.

You have seen how dysfunction occurs in relationships when there is significant drama, when boundaries are not respected, or when good conflict resolution skills are not in place. Drama, a lack of healthy boundaries, and conflict take energy to sustain, energy that could be used to form nurturing and supportive relationships. When our awareness leads us to understand how drama, a lack of healthy boundaries, and conflict affect our relationships, we begin to step out of dysfunctional interactions into healthier relationships.

Getting out of dysfunctional relationships can bring you to a place where you can regain all of the emotional energy expended that can then be applied to the areas of your life bringing you joy and happiness. From this place of strength and clarity, you can set clear boundaries for what is right, not just for yourself, but also for everyone around you.

The void created by moving out of unhealthy relationships creates space for new healthier relationships to emerge. As we begin to attract healthier relationships, we desire engagement with "real" people who are honest and vulnerable and who keep us grounded in our personal presence of truth. Each new relationship brings us the potential for healthier engagement and a new paradigm for how we relate to one another.

You do not have to terminate relationships once you have found your new awareness, but you do have to redefine how you interact or are involved in relationship. You do not have to react to drama and dysfunction, but you do have to choose healthier responses that serve you and the relationships you choose so you can graciously allow them to continue in a way that serves the highest good of all.

As you change and adapt to healthier ways of being in relationship, you will attract different people into your life aligning with your new way of being. These new patterns of behavior bring healthier relationships, and relationships based on dysfunctional behaviors gradually become less

233

important or end. Progress won't be made all at once, but moving forward into healthier behavior patterns and making corrections when needed is all that is required. We lift the consciousness of everyone when we personally raise our own consciousness.

How you connect with yourself affects how you connect with the world. If you are disconnected from yourself, then you disconnect more from others. If you demean yourself, then in turn you will not be able to genuinely honor and respect others. If you do have a high degree of self-love and self-respect, then you reflect this outwardly in how you view and treat others. Climate change around you begins with changes to the inner climate of your love and intimacy.

Becoming a responsible *Adult* is about clearing the unnecessary burden and wasted energy spent on dysfunctional ways of relating, ways that no longer serve oneself and life on earth. In this clearing, we can live a joyful and vibrant existence in harmony with all of life. A critical mass of people awakening is needed to make changes to the world in which we live, and it all begins within ourselves and with our interactions in relationships. Personal responsibility requires we make conscious choices that support and nurture everyone through each interaction.

Each of us now carries a personal responsibility for our personal evolution and invocation to EVOLVE.

About the EVOLVE Series

Never before in history has humankind been faced with decisions as difficult as what is presented now: we either choose to evolve as a species on this planet or reach the tipping point to degrade into complete extinction. The EVOLVE Series of books and writings was conceived to address all that we will face going forward as a human species, but more importantly how we can change the course of human evolution on this planet now before it is too late through each individual taking responsibility for their personal evolution. The companion website http://BecomeAnAdult.com provides more information and resources for furthering human consciousness. You can also connect with us at @BecomeAdult on Twitter, BecomeAnAdult on Facebook, or through email at info@BecomeAnAdult.com. We want to connect and hear your ideas!

The EVOLVE series is designed to look at all of the elements of living on this planet that allows us to share its resources and work together to sustain all of life. EVOLVE will include topics on all aspects of how to effect positive change for the personal evolution of the human species. EVOLVE also uses the Permaculture principles of *self-observation, resilience* and *sustainability* and applies these to all aspects of how we approach and live life on this planet going forward.

EVOLVE is about each individual developing personal responsibility for their life, and then moving outward to change the state of the world around them. Personal responsibility begins when we each accept step in to full accountability for all of our behaviors and actions. To develop personal responsibility, the writings are designed to raise awareness: raising awareness of yourself through self-observation and to raise the awareness of others by bringing truth in to each interaction.

Increasing awareness is key to bringing understanding of how we can thrive is all areas of life and sustain life on this planet. Is there an age where we grow up and become *Adults* or is this an ongoing process? Growing up is not about reaching a certain age of maturity, it is about reaching maturity at any age when we become aware of the areas that bring us into authentic *Adult*hood. This book and subsequent writings in EVOLVE will continue to look at all of the aspects of how we become authentic *Adults* and further inspire you toward developing personal responsibility that brings forth a life of peace and happiness through personal evolution.

Books may be purchased by contacting the publisher and author at:

BECOME AN ADULT, LCC
1001 Bridgeway #218
Sausalito, CA 95421
Email: info@BecomeAnAdult.com

About the Author

Often called a Renaissance man, Steven DeSalvo has a diverse background of creative, artistic, business and personal interests. Steven attended graduate school at University of North Texas where he studied classical music performance. Subsequent to his music degree, Steven worked for Microsoft where he developed his passion for implementing database technology applications to solve real world problems. His passion for the visual arts led him to study fine art and painting at the Florence Academy of Art in Florence, Italy.

Steven experienced a shift in awareness or 'awakening' at the age of 21 which changed how he perceived the world going forward. This experience showed him an awareness of our true nature and connection to everything and everyone, and began a lifelong quest to live in harmony with this awareness.

He has published technical articles for Microsoft and Stanford Medical School, but now works as an independent writer, publisher, speaker and life coach. Steven currently resides in northern California where he plays music, engages in spiritual practices of meditation and prayer, and applies permaculture principles to his daily life. His goal is to serve others in the attainment of their highest evolutionary potential through increased awareness and personal responsibility.

Bibliography

Bern, Eric. Games People Play: The Basic Handbook of Transactional Analysis. Tantor eBooks, 2011

Carus Dr., Paul. Karma, A Story of Buddhist Ethics. 1894

Choy, Acey. "The Winner's Triangle." Transactional Analysis Journal, Vol 20 No. 1, January 1990 (Downloadable PDF for a fee from the *Transactional Analysis Journal*: http://tax.sagepub.com/content/20/1/40.full.pdf.)

Course In Miracles Society. A Course in Miracles, Original Edition Text, Pocket Edition, 2009.

Eldridge, Susan LCSW. "The Healthy Triangle." Whitepaper, 2010, (The Healthy Triangle was modified to include **D**ecisive and **E**mpathetic to align with the meaning presented.)

Harris M.D., Thomas A. I'm OK-You're OK., 1967

Hemenway, Toby. Gaia's Garden, 2009.

Karpman, M.D., Stephen B. "Fairy Tales and Script Drama Analysis," 1968. (Drama Triangle used with permission.)

Kumarappa, Bharatan. Gandhiji's Autobiography (Abridged), 1951, http://www.mkgandhi.org/ebks/AbridgedAutobiography.pdf, Navajivan Publishing House

Mollison, Bill. PERMACULTURE: A Designer's Manual, Second edition, Tagari Publications, 2009

The Holy Bible: King James version. Ivy Books – 1991

Wilkins, Eliza Gregory. *"Know Thyself" In Greek And Latin Literature*. 1979, New York: Garland Pub.

Notes